D0111392

DIALOGUES

— ON —
RACE

SPARK
HOUSE

@2019 Sparkhouse. All rights reserved. Except for brief quotations in critical articles or review, no part of this work may be reproduced without the written permission of the publisher. For inquiries regarding permission contact the publisher's copyright administrator at copyright@1517.media.

Printed in the United States

25 24 23 22 21 20   4 5 6 7 8

ISBN 9781506454023

Written by Kristofer Coffman, Curtiss DeYoung, Lenny Duncan, Broderick Greer, Daniel Hill, Jim Bear Jacobs, Cami Jones, Rozella Haydée White

Edited by Leigh Finke
Cover design by Joe Reinke
Art Direction by Joe Reinke
Interior Design by Joe Reinke

DIALOGUES ON RACE

Sparkhouse team: Carla Barnhill, Aaron Christopher, Leigh Finke, Erin Gibbons, Michael Jeffrey, Josh Stifter, Jeremy Wanek, Erik Ullestad

Unless otherwise noted, all Scripture quotations are from the New Revised Standard Version of the Bible, Copyright ©1989 by the Division of Education of the National Council of Churches of Christ in the United States of America. Used by permission. All rights reserved.

PUBLISHED BY SPARKHOUSE
510 Marquette Avenue
Minneapolis, MN 55402
wearesparkhouse.org

TABLE OF CONTENTS

FOREWORD
BY CURTISS DEYOUNG

Twenty years into the twenty-first century, racism remains central to dialogue in the United States and in faith communities. This century has seen a multiracial coalition elect the first black president of the United States. Then eight years later, we saw a racially polarized electorate that included white nationalists in the voting process elect a white man of an earlier generation. The violence of white supremacy has invaded places of worship, politics, and the streets of towns and cities.

Racial segregation in churches remains entrenched. Most white Christians have very few meaningful contacts with Christians of color. This reality is even more problematic as racial diversity increases in the United States. In twenty-five years, whites will drop below 50% of the population. This demographic trend is already apparent in schools, youth groups, media, popular culture, and political elections.

Discussions of racism now intersect with other conversations on diversity, equity, and inclusion. Addressing racism intersects with LGBTQ realities, #MeToo accountability, and interfaith expressions. Issues prominent in dialogues on race include environmental justice, immigration, and treaty rights for indigenous people of the Americas. Yet the unique features of anti-black racism remain central to discussion.

Today, dialogues on race are as apt to occur in street protests as they are in church basements or coffee shops. Actions and words are not seen as separate encounters. There is an expectation that your personal life and your organization's structural reality are transforming and moving toward the justice that your values and faith call you to proclaim. *Dialogues On: Race* offers a range of perspectives coming from Christian leaders at the front lines of conversation and action in the United States. This book will equip its readers with insights and action steps leading to engagement in the work of racial justice. The chapters that follow are written to educate, challenge, motivate, and empower white Christians to fully enter the dialogue.

Why do white Christians need to do this work? The integrity of the biblical faith we claim must match the faith we live in our daily interactions. The rapid demographic changes are changing our schools, workplaces, and neighborhoods, and we need greater cultural competency and racial understanding to inhabit these places. The future of our country and the world are dependent on the success of this work.

What is required of white people to do this work? Whites must see this dialogue as a priority. We cannot leave the conversation when it feels uncomfortable or we discover our ignorance. Racism is deeply woven throughout all segments of our lives. We must not minimize or deny this reality. Just because we cannot see it or understand it does not mean it is not real. We will need to learn how to recognize systems of racism and acknowledge how these structures have benefited us. We must name these advantages. This may be a painful journey for some. We must persevere through our emotions and feelings and not allow them to block our progress or paralyze our engagement. We cannot expect people of color to do our work for us or provide pastoral care for us when we struggle in the dialogue. And we must pray and invite God into this work of discovery, acknowledgement, repentance, and repair.

This book is a collection of seven chapters covering issues around race, the Bible, whiteness, African American and Native American experiences in the United States, the role of women in racial justice movements, and more. Pastor Daniel Hill starts the dialogue in chapter one with an honest and forthright look at whiteness. He helps the reader understand just what race is and how whiteness emerged. He explains that race (and whiteness) is a social construct rather than an individual's biological attribute or ethnic designation. In chapter two, biblical scholar Kristopher Coffman explores the role of the Bible in the development of racial constructs—while also reminding us that the Bible itself was written before modern notions of racism. He further explores how the Bible navigates difference.

The next section narrates the history and present experiences of African Americans and Native Americans in the United States. Public theologian Rozella Haydée White writes about the black experience in chapter three. She writes with an unapologetic cultural pride and a searing racial analysis as she discusses the history of anti-blackness and Christianity. She recommends blackness as a corrective framework for addressing racism in Christianity. Activist, storyteller, and Pastor Jim Bear Jacobs weaves together personal experience, history, and truth telling in chapter four. He discusses the tensions in being both Native and Christian, the devastating effects of the doctrine of discovery, and the invisibility of Native American life in the United States.

The last three chapters discuss gender and racism, the fact of white churches and black churches, and what is required to embrace a multiracial future. In chapter five, writer and historian Cami Jones delves into the ways that racism interrupts work for gender justice. She also describes the sexism that exists in racial justice circles. Jones reminds us of the intersectionality of this work and how Black women, Indigenous women, and women of color face a double jeopardy. In chapter six, Pastor and theologian Broderick Greer interrogates the realities and dichotomies of a white church and a black church in the United States. He challenges the notion that the church has been serious about racial reconciliation. Pastor Lenny Duncan closes out the book in chapter seven with a call for hope rooted in a reckoning with white supremacy. In much detail, he notes the actions necessary to build a multiracial future.

I invite you to read and reflect on the contents of this book. Dialogue on these matters with others. Commit to be a different person as a result. Then step out into your congregation and larger society prompting more dialogue and working for structural changes.

Dr. Curtiss Paul DeYoung is the CEO of the Minnesota Council of Churches. Previously he was the Executive Director of the historic racial justice organization Community Renewal Society in Chicago and the inaugural Professor of Reconciliation Studies at Bethel University in St. Paul. He earned degrees from the University of St. Thomas, Howard University School of Divinity, and Anderson University. DeYoung is an author or editor of twelve books, including Becoming Like Creoles: Living and Leading at the Intersections of Injustice, Culture, and Religion *(Fortress, 2019).*

1

WHAT DOES IT MEAN TO BE WHITE?

HISTORY AND THE SOCIAL CONSTRUCT OF RACE

BY DANIEL HILL

"If you want to confess your own racism, feel free. But don't you dare accuse me of being a racist. I have never once mistreated a person of color, and I never will. I am not a racist. And I don't appreciate any insinuation that would imply otherwise."

These were the words of a man who attended a talk on race that I gave at a Christian college. They surprised me. I had been invited to be a guest lecturer in several classes that day, and the college had marketed this evening session as a free event for the community. It was billed as "A History of Race," and was geared toward white Christians looking for better ways to understand their cultural identity within the context of the social construct of race.

I had ended the lecture with a closing prayer, and by the time I opened my eyes, this man was at the front of the line, waiting for me to come down from the stage to speak with people individually. I didn't recall saying anything indicating that I thought he (or anyone else for that matter) was an overt racist, but that didn't change his certainty about what he thought he had heard. He restated his argument a few different ways, with the message remaining consistent: he was not a racist, and he was upset about even a hint of possibility that I was grouping him with those who were.

The heightened emotion of his plea was a clue that something deeper was going on. His response pointed to a broader challenge I have come up against time after time. This man's outrage was linked to his definition of race and racism, and his definition was insufficient.

The fact that he was so concerned as to whether he was being portrayed as a racist was evidence that his definition was rooted in a very individualistic view of racism: that racists are individuals who do bad things, and non-racists are individuals who stay far away from those types of activities. Based on that definition, he saw himself as the opposite of racist and was therefore offended at the implication that someone who was "good," like him, could somehow be racist.

I've been interacting with white folks around the topic of race for quite a while now, and the prevailing definition of race and racism tends to be very similar to his. When you press folks on it, most define racism as essentially this: white people thinking/acting/ doing something bad against people of color. Less extreme versions of racism, according to this definition, include calling people names and engaging in crude humor. Then there are the extreme versions, such as engaging in outright discrimination or affiliating with a violent white-supremacist group like the Ku Klux Klan.

While surely, we can agree that we'd all like a world where more people do good things and fewer people do bad things, such a definition is a woefully insufficient way to think of the problem of race. It is superficial, and it misses the much larger threat represented by race and racism.

In her book *So You Want to Talk About Race*, Ijeoma Oluo uses an effective metaphor to address the dilemma that arises with the use of insufficient definitions of racism:

How we define racism also determines how we battle it. If we have cancer and it makes us vomit, we can commit to battling nausea and say we're fighting for our lives, even though the tumor will likely still kill us. When we look at racism simply as "any racial prejudice" we are entered into a battle to win over the hearts and minds of everyone we encounter—fighting only the symptoms of the cancerous system, not the cancer itself. This is not only an impossible task, it's a pretty useless one. Getting my neighbor to love people of color might make it easier to hang around him, but it won't do anything to combat police brutality, racial income inequality, food deserts, or the prison industrial complex.[1]

As I listened to the man at my presentation make his case that he was not a racist, I couldn't help but think of Oluo's metaphor of battling nausea as a means to defeat cancer. His version of "battling nausea" was portrayed differently—befriending people of color, signing up for causes that reflected his value system, and refraining from use of words that could be misperceived as racist. While I'm sure his intentions were sincere, he was missing the larger point. By associating his individual acts of kindness with the fighting of racism, he embodied the very thing Oluo warns about.

If we are going to move past superficial treatments for a profoundly serious problem, we need to get clear on at least three questions: What is race? Why was race created? And what does it mean to be white?

WHAT IS RACE?

My journey into racial awakening began in my early twenties while I worked at a predominantly white megachurch in the suburbs of Chicago. This awakening should have happened much sooner in my life, but finally, the enormous role race plays in the structure of society became apparent to me. As a result, I also began to realize just how naïve and ignorant I had been about race until then. So I set off on a journey to better understand race, racism, and my own whiteness.

I deliberately sought out mentors who could help me better understand race. These mentors told me that if I ever hoped to gain a deeper understanding of race, I would first need to wrap my head around a concept that usually proved complicated for people just starting out on the journey of racial awakening: *race as a social construct.*

Right off the bat, I struggled with the fact that this idea seemed to contradict my religious beliefs about the origin of humankind. As a Christian minister, I held to a deep conviction that God was the author of life, and the creation of human beings was an inherently divine function. How was I to reconcile the idea that race was a socially created construct with my belief that humankind was created by God?

Fortunately, my mentors were patient with me. They helped me see that *both* of these propositions were true. They affirmed the notion that God is the creator of humankind and that humanity bears the image of the Divine. But there is also a humanly created system—the social construct of race. In fact, seeing the link between the two is one of the clearest ways to see the danger of race. It wasn't one or the other, but instead, a clear window into one of the greatest contests between the will of (some) people and the will of God.

To reach a substantial conclusion to the question "What is race?" I have found it crucial to start by sorting out our language. While a number of factors can muddy the waters about race, one of the primary sources of confusion is the multitude of words we use to describe race: *culture, ethnicity, nationality, race, country of origin.* And from there we get the "multi-" words—*multicultural, multiethnic, multiracial*—that further stir up confusion.

To get clear on what race is and why the concept of race is so dangerous, we first need to separate these words into distinct categories. For the sake of simplicity, we'll call the first category *ethnicity*.

When we talk about ethnicity, we're describing the way people identify with each other based on commonalities such as language, history, ancestry, nationality, customs, cuisine, and art. While the cultures that emerge from these collective commonalities are imperfect, ethnicity is nonetheless a reflection of God's image and likeness. Moreover, it seems clear from biblical wisdom that ethnic differences are not just something we experience on earth—they remain part of our resurrected and redeemed experience in eternity. In Revelation 7:9, when describing the nature of humankind in the resurrected state, the author says, "After this I looked, and there was a great multitude that no one could count, from every nation, from all tribes and peoples and languages, standing before the throne and before the Lamb."

When we talk about the second category, *race*, we are describing something very different than ethnicity. Race was created as a social construct to categorize and differentiate people based on *perceived* biological differences deemed by society to be socially significant. There is no scientific basis for distinguishing groups of people based on race, yet scientific knowledge has made almost no headway in stopping the widespread structuring of society around these perceived differences.

What makes the social construct of race so dangerous is that it is essentially a caste system. The assigned differences between races do not leave people on equal footing—some "races" are considered superior; others, fundamentally inferior. Race, then, is a social construct that organizes human beings into social categories based on perceived biological differences, assigning judgments of superiority or inferiority to those groups of people along the way.

WHY WAS RACE CREATED?

The question of why race was created takes us into some of the darkest chapters in our nation's history. When Europeans first colonized America, the concept of race, as we know it today, did not fully exist. The identity of European immigrants was tied to their ethnic and national origin. When they first arrived in America, they weren't referred to as white—they were instead called French, or Italian, or Irish, or Polish. The notion that you could somehow compress all of these diverse cultures into a single label would have sounded ludicrous at the time. Still, European immigrants craved economic opportunities and in order for those to develop, a horrible and immoral infrastructure was required—and this infrastructure could not work without the creation of race.

First, this economic engine required the dispossession of the land occupied by native people. The ongoing draw of Europeans to America was the promise of "free" land, from sea to shining sea. Some early European colonists formed economic partnerships with native communities, but others participated in bloody conflict with native populations. Eventually, such conflict was the common policy of the rapidly expanding colonial effort. If settlers could have acknowledged the humanity of those who already lived here, as well as their expertise in agriculture and caring for the land, the story would almost certainly have been different. Perhaps the newcomers and the native peoples might have formed an economic partnership of some sort.

But that is not what happened. The colonial era unleashed a reign of terror, and native people endured an onslaught of massacres, military occupations, removal from ancestral territories, sexual abuse, forced removal of their children to boarding schools, and disease. These atrocities decimated native populations. By the close of the Indian Wars in the late nineteenth century, fewer than 238,000 indigenous people remained, a sharp decline from the estimated five million to fifteen million living in North America when Columbus arrived in 1492.[2]

This colonialism was inexorably linked to the creation of race. The displacement and genocide of native peoples, much like the slave trade that would follow, created a moral dilemma of epic proportions. How could these new settlers—many of whom were self-identified Christians—justify such barbaric treatment of those who lived here first?

It would be hard to find a more comprehensive answer than the creation of race and the lies that sustained that system. At the core of the social construct of race was the need for a narrative that would justify the settlers' maltreatment of indigenous people. This carefully crafted story contrasted the humanity of the settlers, who were supposedly destined by God to possess the land, and the purported savagery of the native people, who, it was asserted, were dangerous and therefore needed to be conquered.

The Declaration of Independence illustrates this narrative. One of the most celebrated lines in the document that established our nation is its articulation of the following fundamental ideas: "We hold these Truths to be self-evident, that all Men are created equal, that they are endowed by their Creator with certain unalienable Rights, that among these are Life, Liberty, and the Pursuit of Happiness."[3] But the same document later states: "[The present King of Great-Britain] . . . has endeavoured to bring on the Inhabitants of our Frontiers, *the merciless Indian Savages*, whose known Rule of Warfare, is an undistinguished Destruction, of all Ages, Sexes and Conditions" (emphasis added).[4] It must be pointed out that "Inhabitants of our Frontiers" refers to the colonizers, not to the indigenous peoples.

To reiterate: In order to justify colonialism, the Europeans created a story depicting native people as fundamentally dangerous—a narrative positioning them as a permanent threat to the emerging republic. To achieve that aim, our founders used inflammatory terms like "merciless" and "savage" to discredit the humanity of native peoples.

This was not the only instance in which the social construct of race was used to justify and validate behaviors that would otherwise be considered barbaric. The American economic project didn't just require free land—it was predicated on the need for an unpaid labor force. The insatiable appetite for free labor fueled the rapid ascension of the transatlantic slave trade.

Over a 300-year period the transatlantic slave trade transported an estimated eleven million Africans to the Americas in one of the most astonishing forced human migrations in history. Everything about the process was terrifying. It would begin with enslavers marching their captives hundreds of miles to the western coast of Africa, the slaves tied together with wooden yokes around their necks. Then, slave traders would rip families apart and sell them separately to slave ships heading to the Americas. Slaves endured a nightmarish two- to three-month journey across the Atlantic, often shackled together and in life-threatening conditions, all so that the American economy (as well as the economies of other countries) could maintain rapid growth.

Bryan Stevenson, author, speaker, lawyer, and founder of the Equal Justice Initiative[5], is doing some of the most important work in the nation around racial justice. Stevenson trains people around the country on the history of race and how to fight for racial justice. To help clarify the construct of race and how it was created, he introduces an important term: *the narrative of racial difference.*

I recently listened to Stevenson address a group of white ministers and watched as he encouraged them to wrestle with the moral dilemma that slavery represented for white Christians in the early days of America. He said, "These were moral, church-going, Bible-believing Christians, just like you and me. And yet, they somehow found a way to make peace with the incredibly immoral enterprise of slavery. How did they do that? How did they find a way to justify such a barbaric, inhuman system?" His answer: the narrative of racial difference. This narrative provided a story that portrayed race in terms of a human hierarchy. At the top of the hierarchy were white people, who were perceived to be the most human. At the bottom of the hierarchy were black people, who were seen as fundamentally less human. This narrative was believed by slaveholders and non-slaveholders alike.

Here's how Stevenson describes the narrative of racial difference in one of his interviews:

> The whole narrative of white supremacy was created during the era of slavery. It was a necessary theory to make white Christian people feel comfortable with their ownership of other human beings. And we created a narrative of racial difference in this country to sustain slavery, and even people who didn't own slaves bought into that narrative, including people in the North . . . . So this narrative of racial difference has done really destructive things in our society. We created a narrative of racial difference to maintain slavery. And our 13th amendment never dealt with that narrative. It didn't talk about white supremacy. The Emancipation Proclamation doesn't discuss the ideology of white supremacy or the narrative of racial difference, so I don't believe slavery ended in 1865; I believe it just evolved. It turned into decades of racial hierarchy that was violently enforced—from the end of reconstruction until World War II—through acts of racial terror.[6]

The narrative of racial difference succinctly summarizes why European settlers in America and the generations that followed them needed the social construct of race. They were not just looking for a system that recognized racial differences—they needed a system that assigned *human value* (or lack of it) based on those differences.

This era in American history saw the narrative of racial difference encoded into the very fabric of our society. When taxation was being argued between the North and the South during the establishment of the Constitution, for instance, the narrative was accessed to find a compromise. Article I, section 2, paragraph 3 says this about people of African descent:

> Representatives and direct Taxes shall be apportioned among the several States which may be included within this Union, according to their respective Numbers, which shall be determined by adding to the whole Number of free Persons, including those bound to Service for a Term of Years, and excluding Indians not taxed, *three fifths of all other Persons.*[7]

This provision, known as "The Three-Fifths Compromise," would eventually be overturned by the Fourteenth Amendment, but when the Constitution referred to African Americans as three-fifths human, it served as one of the clearest historical examples of the narrative of racial difference: White people were 100 percent human, but black people were only 60 percent human.

The lie of the narrative of racial difference—that there is such a thing as racial superiority and inferiority, and that human value is tied to it—is the ultimate reason white Christians were able to justify and normalize slavery. The narrative of racial difference was so potent that it overpowered the biblical call to view all human beings as equal in the eyes of God.

THE INVENTION OF WHITENESS

While much can and must be said about whiteness, in this section I will explore what it means to be white through the lens of the two questions we have already addressed: What is race? (A social construct.) Why was race created? (To establish a social hierarchy.)

I have been on a journey to understand whiteness for more than twenty years now and have walked with a lot of white folks as they, too, wrestle with cultural identity against the backdrop of our system of race. We must always remember that "white" is not a category created by God. It is a social fabrication. Any white person who sincerely tries to understand what whiteness means for their own sense of identity will experience waves of identity crisis along the course of their journey of racial awakening.

While one essay is not sufficient to fully explore how to overcome this identity crisis, it is important to clarify the roots of the crisis. Earlier, I contrasted ethnicity and race, and that distinction can also be helpful for sorting through some of the confusion about what it means to be white.

Let's start with ethnicity. Just about every white person's story in America finds its roots in an ancestral journey from some European country. For me, that country is Ireland. I've come to deeply appreciate this part of my story and have learned a lot about the history, ancestry, customs, and culture of Ireland.

At the same time, I've had to learn the substantial role race played in the Irish journey to America. At one point, the Irish experienced their own version of oppression and mistreatment based on their social location in their new homeland. But as colonialism and slavery advanced, the social construct of race strengthened, and the significance of skin color with it. This racial construct offered the Irish (and others) a pathway out of the experience of inferiority and granted new access to the power, privilege, and dominance that came with the category "white."

This is only a brief overview of the shift from ethnic identity (such as Irish) to racial identity (in this example, white), but hopefully it offers a clear vantage point to why so much identity confusion often accompanies the journey of a white person trying to make sense of the social construct of race. It also sheds light on why a white individual on this journey typically experiences a wide range of emotions. We are trying to make sense of who we are, yet needing to do so within a social construct that was created with the ulterior motive of consolidating power, privilege, and dominance.

For the purposes of this section, I am simply attempting to acknowledge that due to the fabricated nature of the social construct of race, we should expect to encounter confusion and disorientation when attempting to understand our own ethnic and cultural identity. It's also worth remembering that while the identity confusion that comes with being labeled "white" is certainly real, it pales in comparison to the actual loss of lives in black and brown communities. Therefore, I suggest we acknowledge the confusion, but then quickly shift our focus to developing the resilience and resolve to push forward in both understanding and action.

Understanding race as a social construct is a critical starting point. But that's still not enough. What makes the system of race so immoral is not that it sees differences among people, but that it *assigns value* based on those differences. All human beings are created by God and equal in value. When we created the social construct of race, we created a system that values human beings based on proximity to whiteness. That is to say, instead of acknowledging the inherent dignity of all individuals because they bear the image of the Divine, race created a sophisticated set of narratives that told a story of human dignity in relation to where people fall on the racial hierarchy.

This narrative of racial difference is what made the system of race so deadly in our early history, and it is what allows race to remain deadly in our modern society. Making the connection between the past and the present is another critical piece of understanding what it means to be white, and what it means to live in a society that revolves around the social construct of race. Once again, Bryan Stevenson helps us to see the link between the past and the present, as well as the central role that the narrative of racial differences continues to play:

> I genuinely believe that, despite all of that victimization, the worst part of slavery was this narrative that we created about black people—this idea that black people aren't fully human, that they are three-fifths human, that they are not

capable, that they are not evolved. That ideology, which set up white supremacy in America, was the most poisonous and destructive consequence of two centuries of slavery. And I do believe that we never addressed it. I think the North won the Civil War, but the South won the narrative war. The racial-equality principle that is in our Constitution was never extended to formerly enslaved people, and that is why I say slavery didn't end in 1865. It evolved.[8]

This is the task that lies before all of us in modern society: to become experts at identifying what he refers to as "the narrative war." While social progress has been made in certain sectors, without question the narrative of racial difference continues to plague every social system in life-threatening ways. There are abundant examples that demonstrate this impact in the educational system, in the policing system, in the incarceration system, in the health care system, in access to employment that offers a livable wage, in access to healthy foods, and more.

Though the task of identifying the narrative of racial difference lies before all of us, it is especially critical for those of us who are white. Society does not view racial difference through an equal-opportunity lens. The social construct of race was created for the express purpose of holding up whiteness as the epitome of human dignity, and social systems have been created over hundreds of years to protect that narrative. If we hope to see a turn toward racial equality, there will first need to be a widespread transformation in the white community in terms of identifying, naming, lamenting, and eventually confronting the narrative of racial difference.

Critical self-reflection is a difficult task to engage in when you are part of the dominant culture—think of the metaphor of a fish trying to describe the water it so naturally and effortlessly swims in. It's even more difficult to do critical self-reflection when you are privileged with unearned power; it's not surprising that those in power rarely seek to understand why power has been given to them in the first place. But it's a moral imperative nonetheless. The collective soul of our nation is at stake.

MOVING FORWARD

I opened this chapter with the story of a man who was deeply offended at the prospect of being considered racist. The reason he was offended was largely because his view of racism was deficient. Like many of us who are from dominant culture spaces, he saw racism primarily as an individual set of actions: bad, racist people do bad, racist things. Good people don't.

As we begin to interact with the history of whiteness and race, I suggest that we need a much broader and deeper view of racism. Instead of confining our view to individual acts, we need to open our eyes to the original agenda behind the creation of race: to order human value according to a racial hierarchy.

The social construct that is race is a rival to God. It attempts to redefine human value, establishing dignity based on proximity to whiteness. Worse, it has been the defining story undergirding the development of every social system our society depends on.

If we ever hope to dismantle race, we must first learn to see with clarity exactly what it is.

Daniel Hill is the author of White Awake, 10:10: Life to the Fullest, *and the forthcoming* The End of Supremacy. *Daniel is the founding, Senior Pastor of River City Community Church, located in the west Humboldt Park neighborhood of Chicago. The vision of River City is centered on the core values of worship, reconciliation, and neighborhood development. Formed in 2003, River City longs to see increased spiritual renewal as well as social and economic justice in the Humboldt Park neighborhood and entire city, demonstrating compassion and alleviating poverty as tangible expressions of the Kingdom of God.*

Prior to starting River City, Daniel was part of a series of dot-com startups in the nineties before serving for five years on the staff of Willow Creek Community Church in the suburbs of Chicago. Daniel has his B.S. in Business from Purdue University, his M.A. in Theology from Moody Bible Institute, his certificate in Church-based Community and Economic Development from Harvard Divinity School, and his D.Min. from Northern Baptist Theological Seminary. Daniel is married to Elizabeth, who is a professor of psychology, and they are the proud parents of Xander and Gabriella Hill.

ENDNOTES

1   Ijeoma Oluo, *So You Want to Talk about Race* (New York: Seal Press, 2018), 28.

2   Donald L. Fixico, "When Native Americans Were Slaughtered in the Name of 'Civilization,'" History, March 2, 2018, www.history.com/news/native-americans-genocide-united-states.

3   "The Declaration of Independence," Constitution Facts, www.constitutionfacts.com/us-declaration-of-independence/read-the-declaration/.

4   Ibid.

5   Equal Justice Initiative, www.eji.org.

6   Bryan Stevenson, "Bryan Stevenson on Charleston and Our Real Problem with Race," interview by Corey G. Johnson, The Marshall Project, June 24, 2015, www.themarshallproject.org/2015/06/24/bryan-stevenson-on-charleston-and-our-real-problem-with-race#.mvSlNoxoB.

7   "The Constitution of the United States," Constitution Facts, https://www.usconstitution.cc/#1.

8   Bryan Stevenson, "Bryan Stevenson On What Well-Meaning People Need to Know About Race," interview by James McWilliams, *Pacific Standard*, February 6, 2018, https://psmag.com/magazine/bryan-stevenson-ps-interview.

2

CHRISTMAS COOKIES FROM CAMBODIA

THE BIBLE AND RACE IN AMERICA

BY KRISTOFER COFFMAN

During my senior year in college, one of my roommates and I threw a Christmas party. I drew the task of baking cookies, and as any college student would do, I called my mother. Using recipes I had scrawled on scrap paper as she dictated them over the phone, I turned out dozens of *berliner kranze* and *pepperkaker*, classic Norwegian Christmas cookies.

At St. Olaf College, located in Northfield, Minnesota and founded by Norwegian immigrants, Norwegian cookies bordered on required fare at a Christmas party. However, something about my cookies raised eyebrows. The source of the recipes puzzled our guests, particularly the guests who had met my mother. You see, my mother, in both appearance and personality, is quite obviously not of Norwegian descent. In fact, she grew up in Cambodia and didn't arrive in the United States until 1981. So the question arose, "Where did your mom learn the recipes?" The answer: "From my dad's mother." This would have closed the case if only the next question had remained unasked. But because "Where'd your dad's mom grow up?" yields the response "Mostly in northern China, but also in western Norway," the conversation soon went far afield.

Growing up biracial in the United States has given me an eye for tension and contradiction. Having been an immigrant kid as well doubles that effect, both at home and in American society. At home, it's about negotiating two family worlds, sometimes on questions as seemingly simple as whether to serve potatoes or rice with steak (we always compromise and serve both). Sometimes the family questions are bigger, like the decision my mother made to speak English to my two siblings and me—something with notable implications to this day whenever the family gets together and the older relatives talk about us in Cambodian. We can always sense that we're the topic of the conversation, but we've got little idea what they're saying. Outside the home, it was a matter of acquiring the knack for negotiating people's confusion and questions when they can't quite place my facial features, or their request that I "translate" my relatives' sometimes broken English. In both cases, it's the constant reinforcement of difference. It does, however, get right at the heart of this essay's topic: race and the Bible in the United States.

What's the Bible connection here? In some ways, it has to do with a personal peculiarity: I am a biblical scholar. I first took up studying the Bible through the Religion and Classics departments at St. Olaf; into that study, I brought the tools for sensing and navigating difference, contradiction, and tension—the very tools that came naturally to me as the result of having been a biracial, immigrant kid. But beyond my academic interests, the Bible has much to do with why my Cambodian mother makes Norwegian Christmas cookies, and why my Norwegian grandmother was a citizen of the People's Republic of China all her life.

As I unwind these modern stories, I'll walk through some ways in which the multitude of human voices that wrote the Bible, spanning some 1,000 years of history, have produced tension within the Bible itself. At times the voices in the Bible advocate for one people's exclusive relationship to God. At other times, voices call for the radical inclusion of all people in the community of God. Beginning with the first European colonialists, I will explore the tension in the Bible between racial exclusivity and inclusivity and show how this dynamic casts light on the abusive use of the Bible in American race relations. However, alongside that abuse, the biblical voices of inclusivity have called American Christians to a different kind of relationship with people around the world. This chapter tells a small portion of that story as well; in doing so, I hope to inspire reflection not just on past wrongs and present difficulties, but also on future solutions.

Before beginning that work, however, it's important to clarify one point: The Bible does not include a concept of race equivalent to our modern American conception. As anyone who has filled out the census or taken a standardized test knows, in the United States we group people into "white," "African American," "Asian," etc. Each of these categories covers geographic areas and cultures that may or may not share common traits. These racial categories are humanly constructed, modern, and fluid. For example, within the twentieth century, Italian Americans have gone from being unwanted immigrants to being classified among "white Americans."

Racial categorization fails to take into account many people groups—for instance, where do people from Afghanistan fit in? Nevertheless, these categories set the terms of the discourse in the United States. In hiring, college admissions, housing, and more, we use race as the category by which we determine diversity. Near the end of this essay, we'll return to the problems this causes in the present, but for now, let's take a sprint through the Old and New Testaments and look at some of the ways the ancient writers categorized people.

THE OLD TESTAMENT

In the Old Testament, two concepts dominate discussions of group identity—one used primarily when the Israelites talk about themselves and one used when they talk about others. When the Hebrew Bible discusses the Israelites, the word in Hebrew is *am* (pronounced "ahm"). It is often translated as "people," as in God's command to Moses: "I will send you to Pharaoh to bring my *people*, the Israelites, out of Egypt" (Exodus 3:10). But *people* is a vague term. To better understand the concept, it is useful to consider what traits the individuals in an *am* share. Three traits stand out: First, the people in an *am* share a common ancestor. In the case of Israelite society, organized along patriarchal lines, they trace their lineage back to the three patriarchs, Abraham, Isaac, and Jacob. While they share Abraham and Isaac with other people around them, it is Jacob, the father of those who moved to Egypt, who sets their ancestry apart. Second, the people in an *am* share a common land. Third, the people in an *am* share a common god. In some ways, *am* mirrors our modern concept of ethnicity. However, while there is a hereditary component to *am*, the common land and common god are what differentiate it from the American concept of race.

When the Hebrew Bible discusses peoples other than the Israelites, it uses the word *goyim*, often translated "nations": for example, "When the LORD your God brings you into the land that you are about to enter and occupy, and he clears away many *nations* before you . . ." (Deuteronomy 7:1). *Goyim* (singular *goy*) carries the same associations of *am*, but with the added idea of "foreign nation." As such, *goyim* always highlights the otherness of the people in question. In both Yiddish and English, the word *goy* has survived to the present day as a word used by Jews to refer to non-Jews.

THE NEW TESTAMENT

Although the authors of the New Testament wrote in Greek, not Hebrew, for the most part they borrowed the distinction between *am* (people) and *goyim* (nations). The two terms used in the New Testament were *laos* and *ethnoi*. *Laos* corresponds to *am*, and *ethnoi* (from which we get the English word *ethnic*) corresponds to *goyim*. However, by the first century, the situation had become more complex.

Much of this complexity came about because the Israelites had suffered under the Assyrian and Babylonian empires, and ten of the tribes of Israel had been lost. The remaining two had been conquered by the Romans and now lived in a province called Judea, from which we get the name *Jews*.

Not only had the rise of the Roman Empire united many different people under a common government, but the migration of people throughout the empire stretched the definitions of *people* and *nations*. As one example, a group of Jews had moved to Egypt, to a city called Elefantini. In Elefantini, not only did they have their own temple, but they also had a temple to Isis, an Egyptian goddess. This group, though they still considered themselves part of the Jewish people, did not share a common land with them and, in some ways, did not share a common god.

Finally, the rise of the Roman Empire led people to define themselves in new ways. In addition to the *laos* (people) that they belonged to, they defined themselves based on their relationship to the Roman government. Most prominently in the New Testament, the apostle Paul, Jewish by ancestry, was also a Roman citizen—a fact he used to his advantage many times (see, for example, Acts 16 and 22). Intermarriage within the Roman Empire also contributed to the formation of new identities. For example, Paul's fellow missionary Timothy was half Greek and half Jewish (Acts 16).

Even though the Old and New Testaments differ in language, they maintain the same basic terminology for people groups. Importantly, that terminology is quite different from the modern American conception of race. While the Bible talks about peoples and nations, it doesn't have any term for overarching people groups, like the word *race*. However, the terms in the Bible are similar enough to our modern ideas of ethnicity and race that people have continually applied them up to the present day. In the rest of this chapter, we'll explore those applications—both the good and the disastrous.

DIVING INTO THE BIBLE

It's helpful to keep in mind that while the Old and New Testaments cover very different eras, the ideas in the Bible can't easily be divided between the Old and the New Testaments. The Old Testament, with its concern for the promises of land and peoplehood, often provides an exclusivist outlook. But this exclusion also appears in the New Testament. And though the New Testament contains many texts with an inclusive view, such texts cannot be separated from their roots in the Old Testament prophets. In this section, we'll encounter six examples from the Bible, learning about their original context as well as about ways they've been used and abused in American history. It may be helpful to review the verses in the Bible before reading each section.

THE ABUSE OF THE BIBLE FOR THE PURPOSE OF EXCLUSION

Example 1

When the LORD your God brings you into the land that you are about to enter and occupy, and he clears away many nations before you—the Hittites, the Girgashites, the Amorites, the Canaanites, the Perizzites, the Hivites, and the Jebusites, seven nations mightier and more numerous than you—and when the LORD your God gives them over to you and you defeat them, then you must utterly destroy them. Make no covenant with them and show them no mercy. Do not intermarry with them, giving your daughters to their sons or taking their daughters for your sons, for that would turn away your children from following me, to serve other gods. Then the anger of the LORD would be kindled against you, and he would destroy you quickly. (Deuteronomy 7:1-4)

Context: As we've discussed already, one of the criteria for being a people (Hebrew *am*) in the Old Testament was sharing a common land. However, the Israelites were the descendants of nomadic shepherds and had been slaves in Egypt. Because of this, historically they did not have a land to call their own. One of the promises God made to their ancestor Abraham was a specific homeland for his descendants. However, that land was occupied by other peoples and had been for centuries. Deuteronomy is laid out as a long sermon in which Moses prepares the people to conquer the current residents and take the land for themselves.

Use and abuse: There's no way around it—after Moses' speech in Deuteronomy, the books of Joshua and Judges narrate the bloody conquest of the land by the Israelite tribes. The even greater tragedy of this text is that its example carried on long after the original conquest. The colonists who arrived in North America tended to read the Bible through a method called "allegorical interpretation," meaning readers interpreted the characters in the text as representing themselves and the world around them. They saw themselves as the Israelites who had been chosen by God to conquer the native people and take the land for themselves. They saw the actions of the Israelites as a plan for the conquest of America.

This led to modern race-oriented claims like that made by Senator Thomas Hart Benton in 1846: "It would seem that the White [*sic*] race alone received the divine command, to subdue and replenish the earth: for it is the only race that has obeyed it—the only race that hunts out new and distant lands, and even a New World, to subdue and replenish . . . . The Red [*sic*] race has disappeared from the Atlantic coast; the tribes that resisted civilization met extinction. This is a cause of lamentation with many. For my part, I cannot murmur at what seems to be the effect of divine law."[1] Combining motifs from Deuteronomy and Genesis, Benton epitomizes the racist views that led to the stealing of indigenous land, the cheating and killing of Native Americans, and the reservation system still in place today.

Example 2

After these things had been done, the officials approached me and said, "The people of Israel, the priests, and the Levites have not separated themselves from the peoples of the lands with their abominations, from the Canaanites, the Hittites, the Perizzites, the Jebusites, the Ammonites, the Moabites, the Egyptians, and the Amorites. For they have taken some of their daughters as wives for themselves and for their sons. Thus the holy seed has mixed itself with the peoples of the lands, and in this faithlessness the officials and leaders have led the way." When I heard this, I tore my garment and my mantle, and pulled hair from my head and beard, and sat appalled. Then all who trembled at the words of the God of Israel, because of the faithlessness of the returned exiles, gathered around me while I sat appalled until the evening sacrifice. (Ezra 9:1-4)

Context: Even after they had established themselves as a people, the Israelites found themselves fighting with their neighbors over possession of the land. Eventually, ancient Israel found itself attacked by two large empires—first the Assyrians, then the Babylonians. The Assyrians conquered the ten northern tribes and scattered them throughout their empire. The Babylonians overthrew the Assyrians and then conquered the two remaining tribes, Judah and Benjamin. They took the leaders of Judah and Benjamin into exile in Babylon. After the people were allowed to return to the land of Judah, they looked for an explanation for God having allowed the exile. The priest Ezra decided that the reason f or the punishment was that Israelite men had married foreign women. He tried to "purify" the people by making the men divorce their foreign wives.

Use and abuse: Just as with the Deuteronomy narrative, trouble came about when readers saw the text from Ezra as an example to be followed, not a piece of history to avoid repeating. Notoriously, Ezra 9 became a standard part of the argument for laws restricting interracial marriage, so-called anti-miscegenation laws. Thankfully, after the US Supreme Court declared them unconstitutional in 1967, such laws no longer exist in the United States. However, there are odd remnants of the bias against mixing between races. For instance, when I was growing up in California, the standardized tests that we took also collected demographic data. In the demographic portion, the instructions clearly stated to pick one race only, forcing me to choose on any given day whether I felt more white or more Asian.

Example 3

Slaves, obey your earthly masters with fear and trembling, in singleness of heart, as you obey Christ; not only while being watched, and in order to please them, but as slaves of Christ, doing the will of God from the heart. Render service with enthusiasm, as to the Lord and not to men and women, knowing that whatever good we do, we will receive the same again from the Lord, whether we are slaves or free. (Ephesians 6:5-8)

Context: Fast-forwarding several centuries to the New Testament, we find the biblical author Paul planting new churches in the midst of the diverse society of the Roman Empire. Importantly, Paul held a belief that many Christians today would find peculiar: Paul believed that Christ would return within his lifetime and that the world as he knew it would end. When his congregations asked him for advice on how to organize their lives, Paul always responded with that belief in mind. One of the social realities of the Roman Empire was slavery, and Paul addressed the topic in a letter to a congregation in Ephesus, modern-day Turkey. Paul's reasoning was simple: Christ was coming back very soon, and the world would end; thus, overturning the social order was not important.

Use and abuse: Within the American context, Paul's thoughts on the end of the world were forgotten or ignored. Taking Paul's words out of this context, slave owners cited them as evidence that slavery was an institution ordained by God, a distortion that has long plagued American racial discourse. It is important to recognize that the difference between Paul and American slave owners had nothing to do with "how bad" slavery was or even with slavery's racial dimension. Slavery in the Roman Empire was just as brutal as in the American system. In addition, there was often an ethnic component to Roman slavery, as the Romans enslaved conquered nations. The difference hinged on Paul's apocalyptic worldview and his firm belief that the world was coming to an end. Paul felt that God would take care of the problem, so he advised slaves not to take matters into their own hands. American slave owners, on the other hand, used his words to racist ends, justifying the continued existence of an abhorrent institution, extending it from generation to generation.

THE USE OF THE BIBLE FOR THE PURPOSE OF INCLUSION

Example 1

The word that Isaiah son of Amoz saw concerning Judah and Jerusalem. In days to come the mountain of the LORD's house shall be established as the highest of the mountains, and shall be raised above the hills; all the nations shall stream to it. Many peoples shall come and say, "Come, let us go up to the mountain of the LORD, to the house of the God of Jacob; that he may teach us his ways and that we may walk in his paths." For out of Zion shall go forth instruction, and the word of the LORD from Jerusalem. He shall judge between the nations, and shall arbitrate for many peoples; they shall beat their swords into plowshares, and their spears into pruning hooks; nation shall not lift up sword against nation, neither shall they learn war any more. (Isaiah 2:1-4)

Context: In the midst of the distress caused by the threat of the Assyrian and Babylonian empires, a group of people known as prophets emerged. These prophets brought word from God to the people, calling them to obedience to God, warning them of coming calamity, and critiquing the actions of Israelite and Judean kings who acted without the well-being of the people in mind. In addition to critique and warning, the prophets brought words of comfort and encouragement to their fellow Israelites. One of these prophets was a man named Isaiah, the son of Amoz, who prophesied during the reign of King Uzziah while the Assyrians threatened his people. Isaiah took the words and the images used by empires to threaten and terrorize and turned them into a vision for the future. In Isaiah's vision, God rules and receives tribute from all nations. Not only that, but God teaches the nations of the world how to live in peace, pounding their weapons into agricultural tools.

Use: To understand how radical Isaiah's vision is, we need to return for a moment to the concept of *am* from earlier in this essay. Prior to Isaiah's time, the people of the ancient Near East believed that each individual people had their own land and their own god, neither of which they shared with other nations. While Isaiah still sees each nation as having its own land, he believes that every nation will worship the God of the Israelites and live according to his God's commandments. It might not seem inclusive to modern Americans, but in the sixth century BCE, it shook the foundations of the Israelite nation to imagine that they would share their God with other nations. More importantly, while Isaiah may not have directly influenced the social construct of race for modern American Christians, his vision set the stage for authors of other biblical texts, especially the Great Commission in Matthew 28 and the story of Pentecost in Acts 2.

Example 2

But now that faith has come, we are no longer subject to a disciplinarian, for in Christ Jesus you are all children of God through faith. As many of you as were baptized into Christ have clothed yourselves with Christ. There is no longer Jew or Greek, there is no longer slave or free, there is no longer male and female; for all of you are one in Christ Jesus. And if you belong to Christ, then you are Abraham's offspring, heirs according to the promise.
(Galatians 3:25-29)

Context: The Apostle Paul got angry sometimes, especially when he thought his opponents were distorting the truth. The book of Galatians is a letter to a congregation Paul had planted. After his church-planting, others came to the congregation and demanded that the members be circumcised and live according to Jewish kosher law. In other words, Paul's opponents were trying to make the Galatian Christians part of the Jewish *laos,* worshipping their God and following their laws. Paul attacked this line of reasoning, proclaiming that God's inheritance has nothing to do with human ways of thinking. Humans see distinctions between slave and free, Jew and Gentile, male and female, with one superior to the other. Paul argued instead that membership in God's people has nothing to do with human hierarchies but comes about through God's promise of freedom in Christ.

Use: In response to American slave owners twisting Ephesians 6:5-8 (see previous section, regarding abuse) into a proof text for slavery, abolitionists seized Galatians 3:28 in the fight to free the slaves. They pointed out that Paul clearly states that God recognizes no distinction between slave and free. Based on this, they argued that slavery cannot be an institution ordained by God. The power of this verse didn't fade with the abolition of slavery. Paul not only rejected the slave/free divide, but also the Jew/Gentile and the male/female ones. Civil rights leaders pointed to Galatians 3:28 as an argument against racial segregation and gendered hierarchies, and it has continued to resonate wherever Christians seek to unite across dividing lines.

Example 3

All of them were filled with the Holy Spirit and began to speak in other languages, as the Spirit gave them ability. Now there were devout Jews from every nation under heaven living in Jerusalem. And at this sound the crowd gathered and was bewildered, because each one heard them speaking in the native language of each. Amazed and astonished, they asked, "Are not all these who are speaking Galileans? And how is it that we hear, each of us, in our own native language? Parthians, Medes, Elamites, and residents of Mesopotamia, Judea and Cappadocia, Pontus and Asia, Phrygia and Pamphylia, Egypt and the parts of Libya belonging to Cyrene, and visitors from Rome, both Jews and proselytes, Cretans and Arabs—in our own languages we hear them speaking about God's deeds of power." (Acts 2:4-11)

Context: Fifty days after the death and resurrection of Jesus, his disciples found themselves uncertain of what to do next. At the time, they were a collection of Galilean peasants, unsure of what continuing to follow Jesus would mean for their relationship to their ancestral religion and to their own people. In the miracle of Pentecost, the disciples caught a glimpse of the global trajectory of Christianity. From this international interaction in Jerusalem, the book of Acts goes on to narrate Paul's journey to bring non-Jews into the new Christian faith.

Use: The explicit mention of different languages in the Pentecost story has inspired translators of the Bible, beginning with ancient translations into Coptic and Syriac and continuing into the present day. Translation of the Bible has often been the first step in increased literacy among native populations, helping people acquire the tools to advocate for themselves against dominant colonial languages. The story of Pentecost also inspired one of the first interracial churches in the United States. In 1906, led by William J. Seymour, the son of previously enslaved Africans, the Azusa Street Revival gathered together black, white, Hispanic, Asian, and Native American people, united by their shared experience of speaking in tongues. The Azusa Street Revival was notable not just for its interracial nature, but also as one of the first examples of a church where women were allowed to participate in leadership. The Azusa Street Revival led to the spread of the modern Pentecostal movement, a movement that stands out on account of its interracial demographic breakdown.[2]

BRINGING IT ALL TOGETHER

The ways in which the Bible fed into prejudice and malice cannot be denied or forgotten. European colonists saw themselves as inheritors of a new "promised land" and inflicted pain, disease, and death on the inhabitants of North America, depriving them of their land and their lives. In a similar manner, the Bible was used to justify the trading and enslavement of Africans. Ironically, even as the Bible fed into European Americans' prejudice, it also opened them to a world beyond their own country. Inspired by the Great Commission and in the midst of controversy at home concerning race and slavery, American churches began sending missionaries all over the world.

Those missionaries created great tension in American Christianity. Modern studies of the missionary movement have highlighted the damage done by missionaries who lived in isolated compounds and refused to learn the language or the customs of the country in which they worked. Acting in this superior manner, many missionaries forced their own racial stereotypes on the people they sought to convert. Like Erastus Wentworth, a Methodist missionary who called Chinese food "villainous preparation" and longed for the day when the Chinese would embrace forks and knives, these missionaries caricatured natives as savages and contributed more to American imperialism around the world than to anything else.[3] Their work remains a scar on American Christianity.

Further, the missionary efforts of the twentieth century provided an unintended critique of domestic Christianity. Civil rights leaders used positive missionary actions as a mirror to critique white Christians. They pointed out the hypocrisy of treating foreign Christians with dignity, while turning a blind eye to segregation and brutality at home. In the words of Martin Luther King Jr.: "The paradox of it all is that the white man considers himself the supreme missionary. He sends millions of dollars to the foreign field. And in the midst of that he tramples over the Negro."[4]

Another segment of US missionaries worked in the opposite direction. By living alongside people and learning foreign languages and cultures, these missionaries honored the shared humanity of people among whom they worked. Through the pictures they sent home and their pleas to the churches that had sent them, these missionaries helped American Christians see foreign countries as full of people who could benefit from both spiritual and material support, as well as people from whom American Christians could learn. It may seem odd to modern readers to highlight positive missionary efforts in a piece on race and the church. However, it is important to understand the radical change this represented in the relationship of American Christians to people of other races. For example, when the Norwegian Lutheran Church in America organized the speaking tour of Pastor Peng Fu of China during the early 1940s, it was the first time many Midwesterners had ever seen a Chinese person or heard the Chinese language spoken. Not only that, but Pastor Peng Fu toured the United States as President of the Chinese Lutheran Church, not as a subordinate to any American missionary.[5] These experiences did not change Americans overnight, but they provided an alternative vision of interracial relations.

In addition, missionary work abroad led to missionary work at home in the middle of the twentieth century. Most notably, this occurred in the efforts of Christian relief organizations to resettle refugees in the United States. For example, in the years following the Vietnam War, Christian organizations did the vast majority of the work of resettling Vietnamese, Laotian, Hmong, and Cambodian people around the United States. Quite often it was missionaries or children of missionaries who sparked these efforts.

As with mission efforts abroad, the resettlement of refugees led to tension. At its worst, this resulted in the ignoring or ghettoizing of immigrant communities, a situation that has led to stigmatization and prejudice as well as to economic and educational poverty. Despite pledges from churches and organizations to stay connected with the families they sponsored, movement among refugees or difficulties in communication often led to neglect of those obligations. On the other hand, when refugees did not settle with large groups of their compatriots, churches tended to force assimilation, endeavoring to teach immigrant families the "proper way" to be American and Christian.

That's not to say that no good has come out of resettlement efforts. Immigrant communities have changed the landscapes of major US cities for the better, and by staying in touch with those changes, many US churches have had their cultural horizons expanded.

MOVING FORWARD

As is often the case with such an intimidating topic as race and the Bible, we've done a lot of fly-bys and summaries, moving through American history and the Bible in leaps and bounds. Now let's see how everything we've talked about came together in one particular instance.

In 1911, compelled by Jesus' command to make disciples of all nations, Kristofer Tvedt left Bergen, Norway, and arrived in St. Paul, Minnesota, to study at Luther Seminary. Within three years, he graduated, married Clara Sethre (the daughter of Norwegian immigrants to Minnesota), and sailed with her to China, where he would spend the next thirty years of his life. In China, he learned Chinese, worked with Chinese lay preachers, and put his training as a nurse to good use.

Despite being a European missionary, he was not immune to the nation's troubles. During the Communist uprising in the 1930s, he spent three months as a prisoner of the Communist army. He also had six children, one of whom was Agnes Tvedt, my paternal grandmother. Because her father was a missionary, my grandmother was born and raised in Henan in northern China. Her first language was Norwegian, and her second was Chinese. She lived there until the Japanese invasion of China in 1937, at which point she and her family fled to the United States. After the war, they intended to return to China, but the new Communist government expelled all foreign missionaries. Despite the expulsion, my grandmother always considered herself closely connected to China and to the cause of missionary work around the world.

In 1981, when my (Chinese-Cambodian) mother fled Cambodia as a refugee, my paternal grandmother welcomed my mother and her family into her home. She taught my mother how to celebrate American—and Norwegian—traditions, including how to follow all her Christmas cookie recipes. She enlisted her son to tutor my mother's brothers through elementary, middle, and high school—that's how my father and mother met. The close contact brought about by missionary efforts and the shared experience of immigration led to my experience of growing up in a fiercely Norwegian and fiercely Chinese-Cambodian household. It's not an existence without tension. But the tensions have allowed us to see behind the dominant narratives of American culture and to empathize with others who must negotiate the same barriers we do.

Even within one family unit, managing cultural differences requires a tremendous amount of work. It's no wonder the work of racial justice can seem insurmountable to those who feel called to right past wrongs and strive for equality in our society. So, where to start?

First and foremost, no matter your background, learn about your own immigrant heritage. For Europeans, the process of becoming white Americans involved anguish, the loss of culture and language, and rifts between generations. It's important to learn about how the language transition and assimilation to American culture was often forced and painful. A statement like "We were all immigrants once" is a useless platitude without learning about the history of immigration and understanding how it affects present actions.

We should also learn about the role churches played in both preserving and destroying immigrant heritage. A prime example of this is my own Christian tradition, the Evangelical Lutheran Church in America (ELCA). The ELCA came about through a complicated process of mergers, but in the mid-1950s, twenty years before the formation of the ELCA, the Lutheran church in the US was primarily organized along ethnic lines. Unfortunately, several branches of the Lutheran church that had been in the United States for a longer period of time were aggressively anti-immigrant. They branded Lutheran churches that worshipped in a European language as hopelessly conservative and proclaimed that those Lutherans must speak English and worship like East Coast Lutherans in order to be progressive and relevant. They were successful in badgering other Lutheran churches into abandoning their languages and worship practices.[6] Unless we in the ELCA realize our past sins against Lutheran immigrants, newer immigrant communities cannot trust that we will not repeat those actions.

Beyond personal reflection and learning, the church faces an even more difficult task: having the courage to stop talking and start listening to the experiences of immigrants and people of color.. The temptation in the face of such a monumental task is to fill the room with chatter. However, time and time again the primary problem with the American church and the issue of race has been the church's failure to listen. The twisting of biblical texts to racist ends results from failing to listen to the author's voice; American missionaries became colonial tools when they failed to listen to the people around them; immigrant communities, native communities, and communities of color continue to be racialized and ghettoized in cities that fail to listen to them.

There is a need to listen. Not only do we need to raise up different voices within our own churches, but we also need to enter into conversation with other churches, both at home and abroad, that don't share our preconceptions about what the Christian faith looks like. We can continue to strangle their voices with threats of withholding American dollars, or we can have the humility to admit that they have an equal claim to the truth of the gospel. It will take honesty and courage far beyond anything that the American church has shown up to the present day in order to even begin the conversation. But once we begin, who knows where it will take us?

Kristofer Coffman is the son of immigrants from Norway and
Cambodia. He grew up in southern California, but moved to
Minnesota to study at St. Olaf College in Northfield. After St. Olaf, he
earned an MDiv from Luther Seminary in St. Paul and is a candidate
for ordained ministry in the ELCA. He currently lives in Minneapolis
with his wife Julie and is a PhD student at the University of
Minnesota in the Classical and Near Eastern Studies Department.
His academic interests include the parables of Jesus, ancient
agricultural practices, and the translation of the New Testament
into modern languages.

ENDNOTES

1   "Senator Thomas Hart Benton on Manifest Destiny,"
Congressional Globe 29, no. 1 (1846): 917–18. Accessed online
at https://pages.uoregon.edu/mjdennis/courses/hst469_ben-
ton.htm.

2   As of the 2017 Pew Religious Survey, white Americans make
up only 59 percent of Pentecostals. http://www.pewforum.
org/religious-landscape-study/racial-and-ethnic-composition/.

3   Quoted in Ryan Dunch, "Beyond Cultural Imperialism:
Cultural Theory, Christian Missions, and Global Modernity,"
History and Theory 41, no. 3 (2002): 301–25. JSTOR, www.
jstor.org/stable/3590688.

4   Martin Luther King Jr., "Redirecting Our Missionary Zeal,"
King Papers, https://kinginstitute.stanford.edu/king-papers/
documents/redirecting-our-missionary-zeal.

5   Andrew Burgess, *Peng Fu from Junan* (Minneapolis: Augs-
burg Publishing House, 1948).

6   This occurred most significantly in the development of the
Service Book and Hymnal of 1958, chronicled in: Verlyn Dean
Anderson, "The History and Acculturation of the English
Language Hymnals of the Norwegian-American Lutheran
Churches, 1879–1958" (PhD diss., University of Minnesota,
1972), 94. Further information is found in the journals of
Selmar Berge, held in the Luther College Archives, Decorah,
Iowa.

3

SAY IT LOUD: I'M BLACK AND I'M PROUD

ANTI-BLACKNESS, OPPRESSION, AND DEHUMANIZATION OF BLACK BODIES

BY ROZELLA HAYDÉE WHITE

I grew up in an unapologetically Black[1] household, the daughter of Black American parents. My mother is the descendant of Afro-Caribbeans with ancestry rooted in Panama, Puerto Rico, Jamaica, and St. Croix. Her parents were both of Puerto Rican descent and embodied the both/and of Black Americanism and the distinctly flavored Latin@[2] culture that was a product of La Isla del Encanto. Puerto Ricans are a multifaceted people, a product of colonial Spaniards, Black Africans, and the indigenous tribe of Taino Indians. This mix of histories, cultures, and identities comes together to create a population that is proud, resilient, and full of joy.

My father is the direct descendant of enslaved Black Americans—those who were forced onto boats off the coast of western Africa and who survived the Middle Passage: the death-dealing journey that packed Black bodies on ships to be bought, sold, used, and abused as they built the country we now know as the United States. His ancestors were dropped off along the southeastern coast of the United States, enslaved to work plantations throughout Georgia and the Carolinas. My father's mother is the granddaughter of sharecroppers, only two generations removed from chattel slavery.

Both of my parents' families migrated to New York, which is where my story began. Knowing who I am, along with the stories of my ancestors, was a critical part of my upbringing. My Blackness was and continues to be an inextricable aspect of my identity. The skin that I inhabit is not just a color or a race. It holds the story of generations of those who have come before me. Blackness is an all-encompassing concept—one that takes into account skin color, history, and culture. While originating on the continent of Africa, Blackness extends to other parts of the world. Afro-Caribbeans and those from Central and South America who are Black have a different experience than those from Africa, but they are also a part of the Black diaspora.

American Blackness has an additional dimension: to be a Black American means that the culture and identity you claim are directly linked to an experience of enslavement, oppression, systemic dehumanization, and the constant attack on your personhood and body. American Blackness is informed by Jim Crow, the period of US history when segregation and discrimination were legal.

This experience of discrimination and the resilience of my people led to the creation of language, ways of being and knowing (epistemologies), faith practices, familial traditions, art, food, and attitudes—in short, culture—that defines what it means to be Black and American. Our identity as Americans was not recognized in ways that afforded us the same access as white people to opportunities and resources. The fact that we were American did not count for anything. But to be Black? This provided us a foundation for understanding the *who* and *why* of our people in the face of ongoing dehumanization and a system that threatened our lives daily. The ingenuity of our Blackness, which was informed by ancestral lineage and generational stories, led to an identity that represented all of who we are and provided us with strength and resilience.

As a Black American who identifies as Christian, an important part of my faith formation was uncovering the ways in which my ancestors made sense of a religion that was used as the foundation of their subjugation. I have also wondered how followers of the Jesus I profess interpreted their faith in ways that allowed them to take part in widespread oppression.

CHRISTIANITY AND ANTI-BLACKNESS

Whether we like it or not, Christianity as an ideology and practice has been used to justify the dehumanization of Black people throughout history. In countless ways, Christianity has perpetuated anti-Blackness. Anti-Blackness as a concept did not just appear. A confluence of ideologies, philosophies, and histories has perpetuated the notion that Blackness is bad, that Blackness represents evil, and that Blackness is subhuman.

In this country, the most often quoted scriptural example used to justify the oppression of Black people was the "curse of Ham" in Genesis. In this story, Noah was drunk and naked. His youngest son, Ham, saw him naked and told his older brothers, Shem and Japheth. The older two brothers looked away from their father's nakedness as they covered him. When Noah awoke, he is said to have known what Ham did and to curse him:

> "Cursed be Canaan [Ham]; lowest of slaves shall he be to his brothers." He also said, "Blessed by the LORD my God be Shem; and let Canaan be his slave. May God make space for Japheth, and let him live in the tents of Shem; and let Canaan be his slave." (Genesis 9:25-27)

This text is explored in detail in *The Africana Bible: Reading Israel's Scriptures from Africa and the African Diaspora*:

> This text is a passage with one of the most notorious histories of interpretation in all of the Hebrew scriptures. . . . [This] passage was revived and reinterpreted in the seventeenth and eighteenth centuries by Euro-Americans and leveled against a new target of oppression. In this instance, Africana peoples were deemed the "Sons of Ham" and this curse of perpetual servitude was leveled against our ancestors as theological justification for their enslavement. . . . This text establishes a theological precedent for the abuse of an "Other" by a favored group and can easily be adopted as proof text by subsequent groups seeking to legitimate theologically their superiority over or oppression of another "othered" group.[3]

This is why our hermeneutics—the means and methods of interpretation—are critical. The implications of how meaning is made from a source can have dire consequences. This text's use as a proof text for the oppression of people based on the color of their skin—on their bodies—is an example of how careless or malicious handling of sacred texts can do irreparable harm. Because I am a person of faith who was formed theologically and professes a particular version of Christianity known as Lutheranism, the style of my interpretation informs my belief and my behaviors. Because I believe in a God who creates, liberates, and sustains, I cannot imagine engaging in behaviors, systems, or structures that destroy, oppress, or divide. The ways in which I interpret Scripture flow through a belief in a God of liberation. Even when Scripture is problematic and seems outdated, I have to struggle with it through the lens of a life-giving God.

The Christian Bible in its entirety has been used to justify division, oppression, and the creation of hierarchies within humanity. Whether subjugation of people is based on race, ethnicity, gender, ability, or sexuality, any use of Scripture that dehumanizes and demeans another is problematic. We must interrogate our beliefs and our behaviors if they do not view every person as a child of God, fearfully and wonderfully made in the image of the Divine. Beliefs that do not affirm this reality are antithetical to the gospel of Jesus Christ. When we read Scripture in isolation and without clarity about the context, misinterpretation and mal-interpretation are bound to happen. In the words of Martin Luther, the Bible is "the cradle wherein Christ is laid."[4] For Lutherans, this means that Scripture holds the Christ-child, and the ways we interpret Scripture cannot be separate and apart from the Word of God in human form—Jesus.

Theologies and perspectives that misinterpret Scripture are responsible for the ways in which this religious tradition has been used to condemn Blackness. Thinking about my ancestors who gathered in Hush Harbors and created space to worship a God of liberation reminds me that the gospel is more powerful than any force of enslavement.[5] While enslaved and abused people had every reason to turn their backs on this religion, they did not. I believe it was their experience of Blackness—their intrinsic understanding of their worth and their formation in the *imago Dei*, the image of God—that superseded their lived reality. If they could claim Christianity as their own, reimagined in ways that gave life rather than dealing death, then I can trust that the faith of my ancestors is a faith worth believing and keeping.

BELIEFS INFORM BEHAVIORS

When a person or population believes that they are superior, their actions will reflect this belief. They will do things to preserve their superiority. If those beliefs represents the majority population, then systems and structures will be created that maintain their interests. Norms and standards that reflect their lived experience will become *the* norms and standards by which everything and everyone else is judged. They will see things solely through the lens of their lives—their culture, their beliefs, and their bodies. When we talk about white privilege and whiteness, this is what we are referring to—a way of being that aligns with the belief that a particular race or group is superior to another and is then afforded privileges reserved for that race or group. This superiority gets embedded in the larger culture and becomes the barometer for how life is to be lived.

And here's the thing about beliefs: They are insidious. One does not have to intentionally do anything in order to believe something. Beliefs can be a product of one's environment, upbringing, or consistent messaging that infiltrates your subconscious. Beliefs can be perpetuated as effortlessly as taking in the air we breathe. Beliefs undergird our actions, whether we are conscious of them or not.

One belief in particular has impacted us all when it comes to issues of race and human flourishing. Eurocentrism, a worldview centered on anything that originates in Western European civilization—culture, philosophy, art, aesthetics, etc.—has influenced how we view ourselves, others, and society. As historian Laxman Satya puts it, "Eurocentrism is a way of dominating the exchange of ideas to show the superiority of one perspective and how much power it holds over different social groups."[6]

This belief—that people and ideologies birthed in Western Europe are superior—undergirded mass movements of dehumanization and destruction. An unholy cauldron that included greed, economics, colonization, and a Eurocentric worldview created an ideology of anti-Blackness. Religion interpreted through a Eurocentric lens was then used to reinforce this belief.

Portugal is one of the earliest known proponents of forced removal of Africans from the continent for enslaved labor. While slavery in various forms did exist across Africa, chattel slavery and the enslavement of future generations because of their parentage was a major difference introduced in the transatlantic slave trade. Beginning in the fifteenth century and lasting until the nineteenth century, the transatlantic slave trade enslaved between eight and twelve million people. Those who survived the Middle Passage were forced to labor in European colonies in North and South America, building the economies of Britain, France, Portugal, Spain, and what is now known as the United States.

The church—both the Catholic church and Protestant denominations—was largely in support of slavery. While there were abolitionists who spoke out against the inhumane treatment of Black bodies, the majority of people of faith were either silent about or wholly aligned with the slavery enterprise. Theological ideologies and beliefs provided the foundation for behavior that decimated a continent and a people. European powers destabilized Africa, and toward the end of the nineteenth century, Europe took control of the continent in what is known as the Scramble for Africa. By the early twentieth century, Europe controlled 90 percent of the continent.

These actions and behaviors were the direct result of an ideology known as European exceptionalism. The belief that those of European descent were entitled to the land and the people of the world had a devastating impact. Religion formed an unholy alliance with the geopolitical realities of the time. As European powers colonized the African continent, overtaking countries, disrupting lives and traditions, and taking control of resources and means of production, Christian missionaries began the work of conversion according to particular interpretations of Scripture and theological understandings. Jomo Kenyatta, the first prime minister and president of an independent Kenya, is famously known to have said, "When the missionaries arrived, the Africans had the land and the missionaries had the Bible. They taught how to pray with our eyes closed. When we opened them, they had the land and we had the Bible."[7]

As all of this was unfolding on the African continent, life for the enslaved peoples in America was unlike anything that had been seen before. Beliefs continued to inform behaviors of slave owners and leaders throughout the American colonies. The rape, torture, familial destruction, and inhumane treatment of those who were enslaved laid the groundwork for a people who would continually be dehumanized throughout the history of a newly formed country.

American chattel slavery was not the beginning of racism. Slavery, legalized oppression, and discrimination were created to systematize racism and enforce the belief that whiteness was superior and Blackness was inferior. Slavery existed in America for almost four hundred years. Generation after generation was born enslaved, with no control over their personhood or bodies. This reality annihilated the dreams, hopes, and visions of more people than we could ever know. The ending of slavery did not end the demonization and dehumanization of Black bodies. It laid the groundwork for a population to be viewed as inferior and to continually struggle for acceptance within a society that never valued their personhood.

FROM SLAVERY TO JIM CROW TO BLACK LIVES MATTER

I am from Houston, Texas, where I grew up celebrating Juneteenth. When I left Houston in 2007, 1 lived in three different cities over the course of ten years. Imagine my surprise when most people in these places (Philadelphia, Atlanta, and Chicago) had never heard of Juneteenth. I was astonished! How could such an important part of American history be known by so few people?

On January 1, 1863, the Emancipation Proclamation took effect, abolishing slavery after four hundred years. This changed the federal legal status of more than 3.5 million slaves. Many, including me, wonder about the intent and signing of the Proclamation. It happened during the American Civil War, and the North needed more people to fight against the South. President Lincoln invoked the executive "war powers" to release the slaves, and to many this was seen as a political move to increase people power for the war rather than as a moral move to grant human beings their freedom.

However, the Emancipation Proclamation didn't reach the people in Texas until June 19, 1865. As Texas was not a battleground state in the Civil War, the initial proclamation did not apply. Slaves in Texas didn't find out that their status had changed until two years after the fact. When the Emancipation Proclamation was shared in Galveston, an island sixty miles southeast of Houston, freed slaves rejoiced.

Immediately upon the end of the Civil War, America entered a period known as Reconstruction. For recently freed slaves, this was the first time the majority of the Black population experienced freedom from slave owners in over four hundred years. One might argue that the term *freedom* could only be loosely applied to the status of the formerly enslaved. Newly freed Black people in the South still dealt with legalized discrimination, and while some freedoms were granted, laws known as Black codes outlined what Blacks could and could not do.[8]

Life for Blacks varied between the South and the North, but some things were the same in both. Across the United States anti-Blackness persisted, and people were denied the full benefits of citizenship and inclusion in American society. Despite the lingering effects of slavery and the unequal enforcement of freedoms, this time proved to be one of community building and support throughout the Black community. The Black church as an institution was born. Segregationist attitudes persisted in the North and the South when it came to church membership and involvement. Reconstruction saw the birth of historically Black denominations: the African Methodist Episcopal Church, the African Methodist Episcopal Zion Church, the National Baptist Convention, and the Church of God in Christ. This marked the first time Blacks had ownership over their beliefs and the practices associated with their culture. The Black church became a safe haven and the center of Black life and community.

Reconstruction also included the development of Historically Black Colleges and Universities (HBCUs).[9] I am a graduate and supporter of these institutions, many of which were started by the Black church. Quality education was needed for a newly freed population, and ongoing attitudes and beliefs about Blacks made it almost impossible for this to happen in white institutions.

During this time and throughout the Civil Rights era, the Black church and religion played a significant role in reimagining the visions, hopes, and dreams of a population whose personhood had previously been denied. Instead of believing the misinterpreted theological and biblical statements of those who had enslaved and oppressed, Black people understood the biblical story and Christianity as a religion for the oppressed—a religion that brought about liberation, healing, and hope for all. This was a revolutionary imagining that I believe was directly informed by the Holy Spirit.

Reconstruction lasted about twelve years, from 1865 to 1877. While the Black church and HBCUs began the work of uplifting and empowering the four million newly freed people, societal changes positively impacting the lives of the Black population did not occur. More than four thousand lynchings were recorded during this time. The Ku Klux Klan, a white supremacist organization, terrorized Black communities. Black bodies were seen as an abomination. Freedom from slavery did not mean that Blacks were free from oppression and dehumanization.

After Reconstruction, the Southern United States entered the generations-long era of Jim Crow, a system of legalized segregation and discrimination. Jim Crow laws required segregation throughout public life. In the northern states, discrimination and segregation didn't have the formal structures of state laws, but Blacks still had less access to resources and opportunities than their white counterparts did. Even though Blacks had been freed, they were still not living the life described in the Preamble of the Declaration of Independence: "We hold these Truths to be self-evident, that all

Men are created equal, that they are endowed by their Creator with certain unalienable Rights, that among these are Life, Liberty, and the Pursuit of Happiness."[10]

The social and legal framework of the Jim Crow era remained in effect for ninety years, subjugating Blacks socially and legally, until the Civil Rights Movement of the 1960s.

Even as gross disparities and ongoing violence against Black bodies persisted throughout the United States, a few key events provided the groundwork for the fight for Black Civil Rights. The outlawing of public-school segregation in *Brown v. the Board of Education*, Rosa Parks beginning the Montgomery Bus Boycott, and the creation of the Southern Christian Leadership Conference all created traction and support.

By this time, well-known leaders had also emerged in the Civil Rights Movement, informed by an intrinsic belief that they were made in the image of God and worthy of respect, freedom, and liberation. "Powered by the belief that all men and women are children of God, they set forth to assure that justice, fair treatment, and equal opportunity were awarded to people of all races, cultural backgrounds, and religious faiths."[11]

This religious ideology differed from that of their oppressors. Instead of using religion to divide and perpetuate false hierarchies, leaders of the Civil Rights Movement understood that religion was ultimately about liberation. As a corrective for the ideologies born out of a population's desire for power over others, theologies from the margins were created to take into account life-giving ways to read and live Scripture—ways that took into account all of who a person was; ways that brought about the liberation of souls and bodies. The earliest of these theologies is Black Liberation Theology, named by the late James Cone. Black Liberation Theology was necessary because "American white theology has not been involved in the struggle for Black liberation. It has been basically a theology of the white oppressor, giving religious sanction to the genocide of American Indians and the enslavement of Africans."[12]

Cone, along with other Black religious scholars, gave us the language for a theological interpretation that led us to see ourselves as God's creation: to see all of who we are—our humanity, our bodies, our Blackness—as divinely inspired and crafted lovingly by God. This reminder laid the groundwork for a rallying cry that is often misunderstood today but that is absolutely a theological and philosophical statement: Black Lives Matter.

BLM: NOT YOUR MOMMA'S CIVIL RIGHTS MOVEMENT

Between the end of the Civil Rights Movement and today, Black people have continued to suffer at the hands of the systems and structures that were never designed to support them. The threads of Eurocentrism, white privilege, and racism create a tapestry of oppression that suffocates and paralyzes. This history is recorded at the Tracing Center, an organization created to increase awareness of America's complicity in the slave trade. According to the Tracing Center, "Black Americans made little progress during the century following slavery, while falling further behind white Americans, and progress since that time has been glacially slow by most social and economic indicators."[13] To believe that the state of the Black community today is not directly tied to the history of Black people in America ignores this clear connection.

In her bestseller *The New Jim Crow*, Michelle Alexander details how mass incarceration has taken the place of the caste-like system of Jim Crow.[14] Black people are incarcerated at higher rates, and rights are stripped once they are "legally" imprisoned. Alexander shows how, even though it is illegal to discriminate on the basis of race, the unholy alliance between for-profit prisons and unjust laws led to the creation of a new system of racial control.

While one might argue that things are better for Black people now, a closer look at the lived reality reveals that oppression and dehumanization have taken on new forms. No longer are legalized slavery and segregation permissible, but mass incarceration, police brutality, unequal treatment of Blacks for offenses similar to those by whites, and institutionalized ideologies about race have taken their place.

Over the past few years, the murder of Black bodies has been prominent in the American psyche. Trayvon Martin, a seventeen-year-old high school student visiting his father, was killed by George Zimmerman in their gated community in Sanford, Florida, in February 2012. Zimmerman was freed based on the "Stand Your Ground" law, which states that if one feels they are in danger, they have the right to defend themselves. Martin was unarmed.

Eric Garner, an unarmed man, was choked to death in July 2014 by a New York City police officer. NYPD policy prohibits the use of chokeholds. Video footage shows us that Garner's last words were "I can't breathe." There is no clearer image of racism as sin than Garner's gut-wrenching death caught on video. I can't imagine squeezing the life out of someone. How do human hands do that? It's only possible if you stop thinking of the person you are killing as a person. In that moment they must become an "other."

As people of Christian faith, we believe that the life that flows through our veins is the *ruach*, which is Hebrew for "breath of God" or "air in motion." God's breath courses through us and brings us to life. Without this moving air, this holy breath, we are not alive. Eric Garner's breath was taken from him. As I believe we are made in God's holy image, I believe that Garner's death symbolized the death of God. To dismiss, discount, and destroy the humanity of another is to kill the humanity that God embedded in each of us, the humanity that God chose to embody and take on. When we refuse to see the image of the Divine in the other; when we dehumanize each other to the point of no return, we engage in the ongoing crucifixion of God.

The list goes on.

February 16, 2014: A police officer ordered Yvette Smith to exit a house in which two men were fighting. When she opened the door, the officer shot her twice, killing her.

August 9, 2014: Eighteen-year-old Michael Brown was fatally shot by a white police officer in Ferguson, Missouri. Brown was shot a total of six times and was unarmed.

November 22, 2014: Twelve-year-old Tamir Rice was killed by police officers in Cleveland, Ohio, as he played with a toy gun.

April 4, 2015: Walter Scott was shot multiple times from behind as he fled the scene of a traffic stop. The police officer responsible for the shooting said that he shot Scott in self-defense. Scott was unarmed.

April 12, 2015: Freddie Gray was arrested in Baltimore, Maryland, for allegedly possessing a knife that was illegal under Baltimore law. Witnesses say he was badly beaten before being placed in a police van. The arresting police officers denied using unnecessary force and said he sustained injuries from not being strapped in during transport. On April 19, Gray died from neck and spinal injuries.

These are just a few of the stories of the killing of Black people that have captured national attention. In 2015, the *Washington Post* launched a study of police-involved fatalities. A key finding came to the forefront: Race remains the most volatile flash point in any accounting of police shootings. Although Black men make up only 6 percent of the US population, they account for 40 percent of the unarmed men shot to death by police in 2015.[15]

While white males have made up the greatest share of perpetrators of large-scale acts of violence in this country, they are more often than not arrested for their crimes, not killed on the spot. When Dylann Roof went on a shooting rampage at the historic Mother

Emanuel AME church in Charleston, South Carolina, on June 17, 2015, killing nine Black leaders and parishioners, he was not only apprehended peacefully—he was taken to get lunch en route to jail.

Black males, on the other hand, are viewed as a threat. Statements from those who have killed unarmed Black men reveal that either a sense of fear or a disregard for the humanity of the Black person led to the fatal shooting.

The Movement for Black Lives and the rallying call of Black Lives Matter were not created to disregard the sanctity of all life.[16] Rather, they were created to bring to the forefront the reality that Black lives have historically and systemically been disregarded, dehumanized, and destroyed. Black Lives Matter is a theological proclamation that reminds us that the Black body and the Black life is a manifestation of God's creativity and is just as worthy as any and every other body and life.

The Movement for Black Lives is an organized movement that includes policy demands for Black power, freedom, and justice. It's not always a nice movement, departing from the often romanticized Civil Rights Movement of the 1960s. The Movement for Black Lives has an underlying urgency propelled by the reality that Black people have suffered far too long. This liberation movement is about the holistic Black experience, and it strives to be radically inclusive of the diversity found among Black people. I am convinced the Christian church can learn from this movement. The church can be made better by this movement. This movement embodies the beliefs of the gospel.

EMBODIED RESISTANCE

I love my church. And when I say "my church," I'm talking about the Evangelical Lutheran Church in America, or the ELCA. I love our theological tenets:

⤷ We believe the reality that we are simultaneously saints and sinners, justified by faith through grace.

⤷ We believe that people are saved by Christ alone and that because of what Christ has done, we are free to engage in works of justice and peace separate and apart from any worry about our salvation. We recognize that what we do earns us nothing in God's economy. We show up and speak out on behalf of our neighbor because we recognize that Christ dwells within each and every person.

⤷ We believe that there is law—that which points out our brokenness and need for total reliance on God—and there is gospel—the good news that proclaims that we are loved and worthy and created in the image of the Divine.

⤷ And we hold deeply to the mystery of the sacraments—that the Holy One shows up in ways we cannot understand, in the ordinary elements of water, bread, and wine, and that this revelation of the Divine leads to extraordinary and transformative power. In these moments, Jesus shows up, simply because he said he would. He continues to keep his promise to us every day.

I love my theological tradition. But I don't love it more than I love Jesus.

Any religious ideology or theological interpretation can supersede belief in Jesus the Christ. Whenever the Christian religion has been used to oppress and divide, it has been tainted and no longer reflects the gospel. Throughout history, Black people have been on the receiving end of harmful ideologies that brought about death. And yet, the story of Jesus is one that continually births new life.

In the Incarnation, we see God proclaiming that the human body matters; that the skin we are in matters. The fact that God showed up as a Middle Eastern Jew who was born to a teenage mother and who lived a life on the move holds meaning for us today. God did not choose to embody the rich and powerful. God came among those on the margins, and God continues to invite us to the margins because that is where the Holy of Holies resides.

So, what if we believed that Blackness offered a corrective framework through which to understand our faith—one that called out and amended the racist, destructive nature of whiteness that informs so much of Christianity today? What if Blackness provided the restoration, healing, and wholeness we so desperately need? What if Blackness was no longer seen as a threat but rather as the mindset needed to usher in holistic liberation?

A theological framework informed by Blackness focuses on three areas: the relationship between Black people and God; the meaning of freedom; and the compatibility between Christianity and protest activity.[17] Expanding this notion to include a focus on the relationships between all people and God has the power to transform human relationships and society. Setting Jesus and the gospel at the center helps us to center those on the margins and the historically outcast as we consider how to embody our beliefs.

We have to reckon with how we have desecrated the body of Christ when we have dehumanized and abused our Black siblings. Turning our attention to the reality of human bodies, the diversity in which they have been created, and the ways that religion has been used to demonize the body will uncover a new way forward, one that recognizes the importance of valuing bodies simply because they are crafted in the image of God. And when we value another's body, we value our own body. When we place ourselves in spaces that seek justice; when we use our voices to speak out against systems of oppression; when we lovingly care for each other, respecting our differences and reveling in our similarities—we honor God in our midst.

Rozella Haydée White is the #LoveBigCoach, one who believes that love and Revolutionary Relationships can heal the world and bring us back to ourselves and to each other. She is the owner of RHW Consulting, which provides life and leadership coaching, retreats, inspirational speaking, and writing that accompanies people as they create and live their most meaningful lives. Rozella actively works to restore hearts to wholeness so that all can not simply survive, but thrive. As a writer, teacher, speaker, and public theologian, Rozella boldly engages issues of faith, justice, self-care, mental illness, and the radical and transformative love of God as embodied in the person of Jesus. Her first book, Love Big: The Power of Revolutionary Relationships to Heal the World, *was published by Fortress Press in May 2019.*

ENDNOTES

1   Writers have various preferences regarding how to represent their identity in print. Several authors in this book choose to capitalize Black and Blackness.

2   Latin@ is a gender-neutral shorthand for Latino/Latina. Learn more at: https://www.noodle.com/articles/latin-what-it-means-and-how-to-say-it.

3   Hugh R. Page Jr., *The Africana Bible: Reading Israel's Scriptures from Africa and the African Diaspora* (Minneapolis: Fortress Press, 2010), 73.

4   Betsy Karkan, "The Cradle of Christ in Every Home: Reformation Translations of the Bible," *Lutheran Reformation*, October 25, 2017, https://lutheranreformation.org/history/cradle-christ-every-home-reformation-translations-bible/#_ftn1.

5   "During antebellum America, a hush harbor (or hush arbor, brush harbor or brush arbor) was a place where slaves would gather in secret to practice religious traditions." "Hush Harbor," Wikipedia, last edited August 17, 2016, https://en.wikipedia.org/wiki/Hush_harbor.

6   Laxman D. Satya, "Eurocentrism in World History: A Critique of Its Propagators," *Economic and Political Weekly* 40, no. 20 (2005): 2051–2055. JSTOR, https://www.jstor.org/stable/4416641?seq=1#page_scan_tab_contents.

7   John Frederick Walker, *A Certain Curve of Horn: The Hundred-Year Quest for the Giant Sable Antelope of Angola* (New York: Grove Press, 2004), 144.

8   After the Civil War, black codes were created to restrict the freedoms of black people and all but requiring their participation in low-wage physical labor. "Under black codes, many states required blacks to sign yearly labor contracts; if they refused, they risked being arrested, fined and forced into unpaid labor." "Black Codes," History, last updated August 21, 2018, https://www.history.com/topics/black-history/black-codes.

9   The efforts of black churches were behind the establishment of the first colleges for African Americans. "The second Morrill Act of 1890 required states—especially former confederate states—to provide land-grants for institutions for black students if admission was not allowed elsewhere. As a result, many Historically Black Colleges and Universities (HBCUs) were founded." National Museum of African American History & Culture, "Five Things to Know: HBCU Edition," https://nmaahc.si.edu/blog/five-things-know-hbcu-edition.

10 "The Declaration of Independence," Constitution Facts, www.constitutionfacts.com/us-declaration-of-independence/read-the-declaration/.

11 Erin Audia, "Religion and the Civil Rights Movement – Background," *Religion & Ethics Newsweekly* (n.d.), https://www.pbs.org/wnet/religionandethics/for-educators/religion-and-the-civil-rights-movement-background/.

12 James Cone, *A Black Theology of Liberation* (Maryknoll, NY: Orbis Books, 1991), 4.

13 The Tracing Center, http://www.tracingcenter.org/resources/background/reconstruction-jim-crow-and-the-civil-rights-era/.

14 Michelle Alexander, *The New Jim Crow: Mass Incarceration in the Age of Colorblindness* (New York: The New Press, 2010).

15 Kimberly Kindy et al., "A year of reckoning: Police fatally shoot nearly 1,000," *Washington Post*, December 26, 2015, https://www.washingtonpost.com/sf/investigative/2015/12/26/a-year-of-reckoning-police-fatally-shoot-nearly-1000/?utm_term=.1fc6ca7f60e3.

16 For more information on Black Lives Matter: https://www.weforum.org/agenda/2016/08/black-lives-matter-movement-explained/

17 Kelly Brown Douglas, *The Black Christ* (Maryknoll, NY: Orbis Books, 1994), 38.

4

AMERICAN AMNESIA

CHRISTIANITY AND THE ERASING OF NATIVE AMERICAN STORIES

BY JIM BEAR JACOBS

Hello, my relatives. My name is Jim Bear Jacobs. You may call me Jim Bear. I am from the Turtle clan of the Mohican Nation and a member of the Stockbridge-Munsee Band of Mohicans. I am the grandson of Gretta Jacobs and Howard Jacobs. I am a husband of twenty years, a father of four, a public speaker, and an associate pastor serving a multicultural Presbyterian congregation in suburban Minneapolis, Minnesota. It is with gratitude in my heart that I extend my greeting to you. Protocol dictates that I announce to you that I speak only for myself. I am not a spokesperson for Native Americans in general, or for my own tribe specifically. Nevertheless, I have been asked to speak to my experience as it pertains to the intersection of Christian practice and Native American spirituality.

I'm willing to bet that all public speakers of Native American heritage get asked one particular question quite regularly. I myself get asked a version of this question at least three times a month: "What am I supposed to call you? American Indian? Native American? Indigenous Person? I don't know what the correct terminology is." One middle-aged gentleman even approached me after a presentation and said, "I know that I'm not supposed to use the word Indian, but that's what I call them." This was not a question but a statement. He was declaring to me that he was going to continue to use his term of choice despite the overwhelming voice coming from Native communities and scholars asking him not to.

My first piece of advice: Don't be that guy. Don't hear the voice of Native peoples and then blatantly decide you do not need to heed it.

The truth is that none of the terms listed above is entirely accurate. The term Indigenous Person/People gets problematic because it brings to mind the original people of a specific area. But because of nineteenth-century United States Indian removal policies, many tribes were uprooted and relocated, and many Indigenous People now live thousands of miles removed from their indigenous land. In my case, the Mohican reservation is currently in central Wisconsin, but that is 1,100 miles away from our ancestral homeland of the Hudson River valley of upstate New York. So even though we are Indigenous, we are not indigenous to our current Wisconsin location.

Likewise, the terms American Indian and Native American are troublesome, as our identities were formed in culture and story that pre-date the very concept of America. As Lakota artist and activist John Trudell said, "We're not [American] Indians and we're not Native Americans. We're older than both concepts. We're the people. We're the Human Beings."[1]

The advice I give when approached with this question is that you will have to do a minimal amount of research to get your answer. When you are referencing a specific person, do the research necessary to learn the person's tribal identity. It is almost always listed in the bios of Native American speakers. Once you learn the tribal identity of the person you are referring to, simply go with that as a descriptive identifier. For example, if you were to reference me in a paper you were writing, you could write "Jim Bear Jacobs (Mohican)." It's that simple, and then you can avoid any awkward confusion. If, however, you are referencing broader cultural concepts or people groups, the terms American Indian and Native American are accepted within academic circles, with Native American being more widely used in recent years. In that vein, for the remainder of this chapter, unless I am specifically referencing my own Mohican identity, I will use the broader term Native American.

THE DEMONIZATION OF NATIVE AMERICANS

I still remember the moment. It was no more than twenty-five seconds, back when I was sixteen years old. But it was enough time for me to learn a valuable lifelong lesson—one with depths I am still discovering to this day.

I grew up in a conservative, fundamentalist megachurch in a suburb of Minneapolis. As a high school student, I was part of the largest youth ministry in the state of Minnesota. Every week our services were spectacular events. Literally hundreds of students gathered to worship, pray, and hear the word of God. This served us quite well, as the excitement of it all generated its own momentum. Every week our numbers grew.

Not wanting to rebel, but still feeling the need to spread my wings, I gained a new freedom when I was sixteen. I bought my first car and no longer had to rely on my mother or the kindness of friends to get anywhere and everywhere. For the first time in my life I was able to travel, by myself, the 250 miles from where I lived to my reservation. I spent that summer break with my grandmother and the rest of my Mohican family. During that time, I started to feel more and more comfortable with how my spirit was breathing among my own people. My body seemed to remember things I had never experienced. Going to powwows and naming ceremonies brought me closer to my relatives and to my Creator. When summer was over and it was time to return for school, a type of melancholy settled over me; I did not look forward to leaving.

My first time back at youth ministry after my summer away held all of the zeal and excitement I had come to expect of time with other

Christians. After the service, I was talking to my youth pastor and telling him about my summer. But as soon as I told him I had taken part in some very meaningful ceremonies, I saw it: His smile turned from genuine to polite but entirely fake. I watched his demeanor change from excitement at having me back to an expression of deep concern. He said he wanted to give me some advice: "You need to remember, Jim Bear, that you are a Christian before you are an Indian. Your ultimate identity lies with Jesus. He is your chief; we are your tribe." I got the distinct impression that with the words *chief* and *tribe* he had exhausted his Native American vocabulary and his understanding of my culture, because after that he slipped into more Christian-jargon explanations about how Jesus is our ultimate sacrifice and we no longer need to chase after insufficient paths to him. The bottom line was clear: the ceremonies where I felt such connection were, at best, unnecessary and, at worst, spiritually dangerous.

For years, I have been on a journey to bring together my Native and Christian identities. In the Christianity of my youth there was no space for expressions in worship that fell outside of accepted evangelical orthodoxy. I have endeavored to decolonize my practice and understanding of Christianity—that is, to separate it from its ties to American colonialism—and incorporate Indigenous ceremonial practices into my spiritual life. This has led me to an understanding of Christ that is much richer and more fulfilling than I had ever previously known. However, it has not been without its challenges. America prides itself on the ideology that anyone can practice whatever spirituality or religion they choose, but in reality, our nation has been very selective about to whom we extend that religious freedom.

The practice of Native American spirituality in the United States was illegal until 1978. Think about that! This country sent people to the moon nine years before it allowed Indigenous Peoples to pray without fear of legal repercussions. This fear of Native spirituality was held in place by decades of systematic demonization of

Indigenous ceremonies, in full cooperation with Christian churches. The downstream effects of this demonization wreak havoc within our communities to this day.

A few years ago, I hosted at my current church a conference that centered on issues dealing with the Christian Doctrine of Discovery. The conference lasted three days and featured many Native American speakers. All our keynote speakers were Native American, most of our breakout workshop leaders were Native American, and though I can't claim that a majority of the audience was Native American, I can state that we had more Native Americans in our audience than most churches across the nation will ever see.

We opened our conference in a traditional way. We recognized the Indigenous People of the land that we were meeting upon (in this case, the Dakota people). We brought in a Dakota drum circle to bless us with traditional songs. And we burned sacred medicines and smudged, or purified with the sacred smoke, the people and the space. After a riveting keynote address by a national expert on the Doctrine of Discovery, we opened the floor for questions and answers.

A Native American man from the audience stepped forward and took the microphone. He introduced himself as coming from the Ojibwe people of northern Minnesota and said he was the pastor of a church in the Minneapolis area. He opened his Bible and read a passage from Isaiah, in which the prophet admonished the people of Israel for their continuing idolatry. He closed his Bible and then addressed me and anyone else in the room who held to the Christian faith: "The scriptures declare that the God we serve is an extremely jealous God. If I was a minister in this church, I would live in fear of God's wrath because you have brought a drum and other detestable objects into the Lord's sanctuary."

I admit that my initial reaction was not very pastoral. I felt a white-hot rage well up within my body. This man—this Native American man—was attacking me in my own church! But after I took a few deep breaths and let some of my elders address the situation, my emotions shifted. My rage was replaced by a deep sadness. I snuck away and hid myself in a dark corner of my church and let the tears run from my eyes.

I wept at feeling the full weight of colonization. I wept that it was so pervasive. I wept that it was so extensive. But mostly I wept that it was so incredibly successful. For centuries Native American spirituality, viewed through the lens of Christianity, was not just unknown and mysterious but was considered dangerous and demonic. The systematic colonization of Native Americans was so successful that here in the twenty-first century, one Native American Christian pastor was ready to call down hellfire upon another Native American Christian pastor for bringing sacred objects into a sacred space.

THE DOCTRINE OF DISCOVERY

Five hundred years ago, during what the history books call the Age of Discovery, explorers from many different European countries set out to discover and lay claim to distant lands in the name of their sovereign crowns. As they did so, they operated under the spiritual authority bestowed upon them through a series of papal edicts issued by the Vatican. These fifteenth-century decrees have come to be known collectively as the Doctrine of Discovery. The Doctrine of Discovery was an agreement between the church of Europe and the nations of Europe, stating that if an explorer sailing under the flag of a European sovereign came across a land that had not previously been claimed by a Christian nation, that land and all its inhabitants could be seized and claimed by the discovering Christian nation.

The first edict that is typically cited as part of the Doctrine of Discovery is *Romanus Pontifex*. Issued by Pope Nicholas V in 1455, it affirmed the authority of King Alfonso of Portugal to lay claim to land in western Africa. It grants King Alfonso the authority to:

invade, search out, capture, vanquish and subdue all Saracens and pagans whatsoever, and other enemies of Christ wheresoever placed, and the kingdoms, dukedoms, principalities, dominions, possessions, and all movable and immovable goods whatsoever held and possessed by them and to reduce their persons to perpetual slavery, and to apply and appropriate to himself and his successors the kingdoms, dukedoms, counties, principalities, dominions, possessions, and goods, and to convert them to his and their use and profit.[2]

By the time Columbus made landfall in North America in 1492, he was operating under the notion that any Indigenous People he might encounter would be "enemies of Christ" whose land could be seized and whose bodies could be reduced to "perpetual slavery." Gone was the biblical truth that all humanity bore the image of God. There were now distinct *us* and *them* categories, and the Indigenous Peoples of the so-called discovered lands were clearly in the *them* category.

As abhorrent and archaic as the Doctrine of Discovery may seem, it is a foundational part of the American legal system still today. As recently as 2005, in the legal case *City of Sherill v. Oneida Nation*, the Doctrine of Discovery was cited as justification to limit tribal sovereignty in a US Supreme Court decision. With European (white) supremacy as the foundation for American society, it is no wonder our collective history is marked by so much devastation.

BOARDING SCHOOL

There is not a Native American alive today who does not in some way carry trauma in their body from the system of residential boarding schools. Almost everyone can name someone in their family who was sent away to one of these institutions. The flagship of the residential boarding school system was the United States Indian Industrial School in Carlisle, Pennsylvania, commonly known simply as Carlisle Indian School. It was founded in 1879 by Richard Henry Pratt.

Carlisle was the first government-funded off-reservation residential boarding school for Native Americans. Children of all ages, from all over the country, were removed from their families, often forcibly, and shipped to Carlisle. Eventually, the funding for such schools would come from a partnership between the federal government and Christian churches. The goal of these institutions was to remove Native children from their homes and purge their spirits and bodies of everything that was a marker of their Native identity. Their hair was cut, they were stripped of the clothes they were wearing when they arrived, and any sacred or ceremonial objects they had brought were taken away. Often these items were burned in a large bonfire as the children watched helplessly.

Pratt coined a motto that would define the ethos of these institutions of trauma: "We must kill the Indian to save the man."[3] In other words, the essence of a child's Native identity must be stripped away and replaced with more socially acceptable (that is, white) alternatives: dress, language, culture—everything.

In 2015, the Canadian Truth and Reconciliation Commission concluded that these residential boarding schools (which existed in Canada as well as in the United States) amounted to nothing less than cultural genocide.[4] The boarding schools left a scar in every Native American family. They are where Native American culture and identity went to die. The trauma from that era is still felt in Native American communities even generations after the initial damage was done. The following personal experience bears this out.

My grandmother lived to be ninety-five years old. Standing only four feet nine inches tall, what she lacked in stature she made up for in spirit. She is easily the strongest and most resilient woman I have ever known. My favorite activity whenever I visited her was to go to her and ask, "Hey, Grandma, do you feel like going for a drive?" She would get excited, and off we would go on an adventure.

Once, when she was around ninety, we went on one of our excursions. They always started the same way: we'd get to the end of her driveway, and I'd ask, "Left or right?" But it really didn't matter which direction she chose because as soon as we left the driveway, her mouth would open and a lifetime of stories would just emerge from her tiny body.

Our reservation in the middle of Wisconsin is just 24,000 acres, not large by any measure. My grandmother spent almost every day of her nine and a half decades within that 24,000-acre space. She knew the story of virtually every square inch of that reservation. At every intersection, I would ask her to choose left or right, and then I would be treated to another wealth of stories. One day, after about two hours of driving, I asked my grandmother if she wanted to go visit Grandpa. I still remember her reply: "I'd really like that. No one takes me out there anymore." You see, Grandpa had died many years prior and was buried in a cemetery several miles off the reservation.

After parking near the small cemetery, I offered her my arm and began to lead her to Grandpa's grave. However, I felt her pulling me slightly in the opposite direction. "Grandma, he's over here," I said. Her reply was sharp: "Don't you think I know where my husband is buried? Come over here. I want to tell you about *this* man."

She led me to a very unassuming gravestone and proceeded to tell me about the man who lay beneath our feet. She then led me to another grave and told me another story. And another. And another. It dawned on me that she knew the story of almost everyone in this cemetery. She told me how, several decades ago, the county had needed to widen the road in front of the cemetery, so they simply moved the stone landscaping wall inward several feet. Then she told me the story of those who remained buried under that wall.

She told me of two brothers buried in opposite corners of the graveyard because they never got along in life and couldn't be trusted to get along in death, so the community made the decision to bury them as far away from each other as possible. For almost a full hour as we walked around, she regaled me with the most fascinating stories—until we finally arrived at our intended destination, the grave of my grandfather. I walked her up to the headstone and then took a few steps back to give them some privacy. They had been married fifty-two years; I figured they probably had some things to talk about.

In the middle of her conversation with her husband, she nonchalantly looked over her shoulder to me and gestured to the horizon—"Over there is where I went to school"—then she turned her attention back to my grandfather. In the direction she had pointed, about a mile across an empty field, stood the telltale outline of a residential boarding school. I knew little about my grandmother's schooling. Everything I did know had come from a middle-school "interview an elder" social studies project. I was aware that she had been sent to live at her school, and that she only went through the eighth grade. That was the full extent of what I knew.

After my grandmother finished up her visit with Grandpa and we returned to the car, I asked if we could go visit her old school. She agreed, and we set off. Even though it was only a mile away across a field, thanks to the layout of Wisconsin's rural roads, it was actually about a four- or five-mile drive there. While we bounced along the country roads, she told me still more treasured stories. As we pulled to the side of the road in front of her school, my first impression was of the buildings' age and state of disrepair. Windows had long been boarded up; parts of the stone façade were crumbling and falling off.

Again, I offered her my arm and followed her lead, taking careful note of how she was responding in this space. Tenderly, she reached out and touched a tree as if greeting an old friend. But upon reaching out to touch one of the buildings, she quickly withdrew her hand before making contact. After about twenty minutes, a sickening realization came over me: *She was not talking! Not one word!*

This woman, who for the last three hours could not keep herself from sharing stories, was struck silent in the shadow of these buildings. After another ten minutes, I quietly asked if she wanted to head home. She pushed a tear from the corner of her eye and nodded. In silence we walked back to the car. After helping her into the passenger seat, I pretended to check something on the back of the car as I swiped at my own tears.

Whatever happened to my grandmother at that school, it stole her voice. Eight decades removed from her time there, it still had her voice. The trauma her body and spirit carried still prevented her from speaking in that space. Apologists for the history of the church will cite the good intentions of the priests and pastors who ran those institutions. They will say they did what they thought was right at the time. But good intentions mean nothing when the outcome is this devastating.

INVISIBLE INDIANS

Perhaps no other group of people occupies such a romanticized space in the American imagination as Native Americans. From the wise sage to the noble savage, images are cemented into the American consciousness. The problem is that when the bulk, if not all, of your understanding of a people group is filtered through antiquated lenses, your view of that people group will be equally outdated and inaccurate.

I want you to do a little experiment for me. Right now, for the next thirty seconds, put this book down, close your eyes, and imagine a Native American. Before you read further, go ahead and do this.

Unless you have a relationship with an actual Native American, chances are that your imagination conjured up a generic Native American straight out of Hollywood central casting: a noble chief in full feathered headdress sitting on the back of a horse, or a beautiful Indian maiden seated by a gently flowing stream as she diligently performs her daily chores.

It's okay to admit that this is where your imagination took you. But we must also recognize that as popular as these images are, they are incomplete and limit our understanding. In most people's imaginations, America's Indigenous Peoples are trapped in the nineteenth century. When most people think of Native Americans, they think horseback and feathers; they don't think minivans and smartphones. This halting of progress in the collective imagination has absurd and damaging effects.

Many years ago, I was asked by a church's children's ministry leader to give a Native culture presentation to their fifth-grade boys. I have done many such presentations. I come in with a wide array of artifacts from my family, explain the spiritual and cultural significance of each one, and usually conclude with some type of cheesy age-appropriate craft project.

But this particular presentation stands out to me because in the middle of it, one of the boys raised his hand to ask a question. When I called on him, he said, "How did you get here?" When I asked what he meant, he responded, "Well, when we came to church tonight, I didn't see a horse outside, so I'm just wondering how you got here today."

I stood in stunned silence for what must have been an uncomfortable amount of time because the boy then tried to clarify his question: "I mean, did you walk here?" I waited for the kid to crack a smile or snicker—anything to indicate he was trying to be funny and making a joke that just wasn't landing. But . . . nothing. He was serious. I looked to the teacher of this group and received nothing more than an eyebrow raise and a shrug.

In this young man's understanding, there was no possible way I could exist as a Native American in the twenty-first century. The lack of a horse in the church parking lot caused confusion that, for him, was legitimate. Nowhere in his understanding was there space to imagine that I had arrived at his location in a high-mileage

Korean import that was slowly rusting away. In his mind, I didn't exist even in the twentieth century, let alone the twenty-first. To him, I was trapped in the 1800s.

Imagine what the reaction would have been if he had treated a guest speaker from any other people group the way he did me. Suppose he had asked an African American about plantation life. We would be appalled that this young man had reached age eleven or twelve and still held such antiquated understandings. We would question the quality of his upbringing and try to determine how his education had failed him. Yet when it comes to Native Americans, these trespasses can be dismissed with a simple shrug of the shoulders.

The fact that in the collective consciousness, the image of Native Americans is largely stalled in the nineteenth century means that our identities can be appropriated and used with virtual impunity. Nowhere is this more evident than with corporate branding and sports mascots. Very often when Native American people offer arguments against or protest the use of racist team names or offensive stereotypical cartoon mascots, they are met with one of two counterarguments.

The first is: "Why are you only complaining about this now? These images and names have been around for decades." People who espouse this argument see current movements to change the image of Native Americans as just another example of hypersensitivity in an age of political correctness run amok. The reality is that Native Americans have been objecting to this appropriation for decades, but until recently our voices were too easily ignored. In our current age of vast social media networks, it is more difficult to ignore voices from the margins of society. Only now are the voices from the shadows really being heard, and to those who have not been aware it can seem like a recent phenomenon.

The second argument appeals to the seemingly good intentions of society: "Why would you be offended? The team chose this name to honor your people." Setting aside the question of how a racial slur or a cartoon image highlighting negative stereotypes could be seen as an honor, I want us to consider a counterpoint to this argument—one that restores and preserves the autonomy of Native American people: Shouldn't the people who are supposedly being honored have a say in what language and images are used to honor them? It is the height of cultural arrogance to prescribe what honors someone else. If the people you claim to honor tell you they are not honored by what you are doing, the only response can be to believe what they are saying and take corrective action. Anything less preserves the damaging paradigm.

In the Gospel of Matthew, Jesus says this about worship: "So when you are offering your gift at the altar, if you remember that your brother or sister has something against you, leave your gift there before the altar and go; first be reconciled to your brother or sister, and then come and offer your gift" (5:23-24).

In these two verses Jesus tells his followers—tells *us*—that we cannot worship fully and freely if our brother or sister has a grievance against us. As Christians, we can have no doubt that some have legitimate grievances against us. The question now is how we go about making reparations.

I often encourage churches I visit to donate to Indigenous language and cultural reclamation projects to begin to repair the damage done by the boarding schools. I urge them to acknowledge that they live on stolen land and to seriously consider returning land to Native tribes. But these are future goals on the road to healing the relationship.

The first step is really quite basic. Paul Chaat Smith (Comanche) says, "If amnesia is the state religion, then the act of remembering turns you into a heretic."[5] The church has intentionally silenced and overlooked the narrative of America's Native people for so long that a full accounting of its sins can never be realized from behind its stained-glass windows. The path forward for the church must begin with building relationships with its Indigenous brothers and sisters, recognizing and valuing the image of the Divine that we have always carried. Sit and listen to our stories of pain and loss, strength and resilience. Fight against the institutional systems that would say we as Native Americans must "get over it."

Fight against the collective amnesia that preserves your comfort, and join Natives in the sacred heresy of remembering.

Jim Bear Jacobs was born in St. Paul, Minnesota. He is a member of the Stockbridge-Munsee Mohican Nation, an American Indian tribe located in central Wisconsin. He has degrees in Pastoral Studies and Christian Theology and has served various churches as youth minister, adult Christian educator, and director of Men's Ministries. Presently he is parish associate at Church of All Nations Presbyterian Church. He is a cultural facilitator in the Twin Cities and works to raise the public's awareness of American Indian causes and injustices. He is Director of Community Engagement and Racial Justice for the Minnesota Council of Churches. Additionally, he is the creator and director of "Healing Minnesota Stories," a program of the Minnesota Council of Churches dedicated to ensuring that the Native American voice is heard in areas where it has long been ignored.

ENDNOTES

1   "Reel Injun," Catherine Bainbride and Neill Diamond, directors (Rezolution Pictures, 2009).

2   The Bull *Romanus Pontifex*, Native Web, https://www.nativeweb.org/pages/legal/indig-romanus-pontifex.html.

3   Capt. Richard H. Pratt, "Kill the Indian, and Save the Man" (speech, Nineteenth Annual Conference of Charities and Correction, 1892). Carlisle Indian School Digital Resources Center, http://carlisleindian.dickinson.edu/teach/kill-indian-and-save-man-capt-richard-h-pratt-education-native-americans.

4   Report is available at the National Centre for Truth and Reconciliation, nctr.ca/reports.php.

5   Paul Chaat Smith, *Everything You Know About Indians is Wrong* (Minneapolis: University of Minnesota Press, 2009), 90.

5

WHITHER THE WOMEN?

RACE, GENDER, AND THE INTERSECTING NATURE OF OPPRESSION

BY CAMI JONES

On the evening of November 6, 2016, I was at the gym. I wanted to get a workout in before the inevitable celebrations for electing our nation's first female president. When the returns started coming in, my fellow gym-mates climbed down from their elliptical machines and treadmills and crowded around the TVs blasting the early vote counts. The mood was darkening, so I headed home where I could refresh the results in peace. I fell asleep around nine and woke up around midnight to the official headlines. My despondency motivated me to spend the night planning what to say to my students, most of whom were brown first- or second-generation immigrants who had expressed increasing anxiety about the election as it got closer.

Some women, like Teresa Shook, communicated their despair on social media. Shook created the Facebook event that evolved into the Women's March. The evolution of the March from a Facebook post to the largest single-day protest in American history was not without controversy.[1] The original name for the event chosen by Shook, who is white, was the Million Woman March, as either a respectful nod to or an ahistorical appropriation of the original Million Woman March planned in 1997 by Phile Chionesu, a Black female activist.[2]

Many were angered not only by the potential co-opting of an event that was originally created for and by Black women, but also by the lack of representation of women of color in the March's leadership. While Linda Sarsour, Tamika Mallory, and Carmen Perez, all women of color, were eventually made co-chairs of the event, in the eyes of many Black women irreparable damage had already been done.

Many Black female activists wrote about why they would not be attending the march, citing their discomfort with the fact that over half of white women who voted in the election had cast their ballots for the candidate who embodied everything the marchers claimed to oppose. Others pointed out the fact that when they attempted to discuss the issues that defined their activism—issues that had a disproportionate impact on Black people in general and Black women in particular—they were shouted down for being divisive.

Cultural critic Jamilah Lemieux, describing her decision not to attend the March, wrote: "I'd like to see a million White women march to the grave of Harriet Tubman, Sojourner Truth or Audre Lorde, or perhaps to the campus of Spelman College to offer a formal apology to Black women. It's time for White women to come together and tell the world how their crimes against Black women, Black men and Black children have been no less devastating than the ones committed by their male counterparts."[3] According to Lemieux, white women had not adequately addressed the history of white women allying with white-supremacist causes, or the present reality that 53 percent of white women had voted for Trump. She felt that her participation in the Women's March would signal a solidarity she did not yet feel. It seemed to her that white women were rushing to reconciliation without having done any of the necessary work to identify and address the wrongs that had been done.

Despite sharing many of those same hesitations, I decided to attend the march in San Francisco on inauguration weekend. I went with some friends from church, and I was, as usual, the only Black person in the group. For the most part, I enjoyed the event. The signs were hilarious, and there was a sense of joy in the air that I hadn't felt since the election results were announced.

In the days following the march, as I reflected on my feelings, read some more articles, and saw some more images, I began to feel a little different. One of the most resonant images I saw was of a woman named Angela Peoples standing in front of a group of white women in pink hats who were gleefully taking a selfie. Peoples stood holding a sign that said "Don't forget: White women voted for Trump," while sucking on a lollipop. That image captured so much of what I had felt at the march but hadn't been able to name until days later. There were so many white women at the Women's March in San Francisco, especially compared to the numbers at other vigils and marches I had attended.

I experienced a mixture of emotions. On the one hand, I felt excitement that so many people were willing to spend a Saturday morning standing against a new administration and its policies. On the other hand, I was suspicious of the motives of my fellow marchers. Were these women planning to show up in droves for future vigils for Black people shot by the police? Would they initiate tough conversations with their friends and family members about their support for Trump and his policies? Would they interrogate their own biases and complicity in the racism and xenophobia that Trump had ridden into office like a wave? During the march, I found myself side-eyeing my fellow marchers, women with pink hats and clever signs, wondering if they were in it for the right reasons or just for the social media capital. Those feelings compounded in the days that followed.

BLACK WOMEN AND THE SUFFRAGE MOVEMENT

The discomfort I felt during the Women's March has been felt by Black American women since the movement to abolish slavery, if not longer. The abolition movement and the women's suffrage movement overlapped from the very beginning. The suffrage movement essentially began when Susan B. Anthony and Elizabeth Cady Stanton, both deeply involved in anti-slavery work, were barred from speaking at the World Anti-Slavery Convention in 1840 because they were women. The first wave of feminism began when they decided to respond to that snub by having their own convention, the Seneca Falls Convention, eight years later.[4]

During that convention, the Declaration of Sentiments was created, which detailed very clearly that women were equal to men and deserved full equality under the law. In an early example of the powerful alliance between the leaders of the contemporary, interdependent movements of women and Black people, Frederick Douglass, longtime friend of Susan B. Anthony, attended and spoke at the Seneca Falls Convention, and signed the Declaration of Sentiments.[5]

That alliance was frayed when it became clear that Black men would be enfranchised before white women. The Fourteenth Amendment, passed during the Reconstruction period and designed to give citizenship rights to previously enslaved Black people, explicitly limited the right to vote to men. The Fifteenth Amendment goes a step further, forbidding the government from preventing a citizen from voting due to his "race, color, or previous condition of servitude."[6] Instead of perceiving this increased enfranchisement as a win for the women's suffrage movement and continuing to fight for the rights of all women to vote, many white suffragists, including Anthony, felt betrayed and began to look elsewhere for support for their movement.[7]

In response to the idea that Black men would receive the vote before white women, Anthony said:

> What words can express [white women's] humiliation when, at the close of this long conflict, the government which she had served so faithfully held her unworthy of a voice in its councils, while it recognized as the political superiors of all the noble

women of the nation the negro men just emerged from slavery, and not only totally illiterate, but also densely ignorant of every public question. . . . The old anti-slavery school says women must stand back and wait until the negroes shall be recognized. But we say, if you will not give the whole loaf of suffrage to the entire people, give it to the most intelligent first. If intelligence, justice, and morality are to have precedence in the government, let the question of the woman be brought up first and that of the negro last.[8]

Instead of focusing her anger at the systems and institutions that continued to deny women the vote, Anthony aimed it at Black men. Her ire that they had received the vote before white women was not based on a belief in equal rights for all; it was based on white supremacy. Some historians argue that this pivot was strategic for Anthony rather than an expression of a change in her personal beliefs about Black rights, but either way, her statement was damaging, as was her later work with white supremacists.[9]

This shift explains, in part, my discomfort when many women placed their "I Voted" stickers on Anthony's grave on November 6, 2016. Anthony notably cast an illegal ballot in the 1872 presidential election. She was arrested and tried, although she refused to pay her fine, calling it an "unjust penalty," again bringing national attention to the women's suffrage movement.[10] Anthony deserves to be remembered for her contributions in the struggle for women's rights, but when she is celebrated and memorialized by predominantly white women, it creates the same suspicion I felt during the Women's March—a suspicion that caused me to be wary of my fellow marchers. Instead of covering the grave of a problematic fave like Susan B. Anthony, we could honor the contributions of Black suffragists and lay tributes at their oft-forgotten graves.

After the Women's March in 2018, the Harriet Tubman statue in Harlem was seen sporting one of the ubiquitous pink hats. Black Twitter responded with a resounding "No!" and the image of Tubman with the knitted pink cap began to represent, for me, the ahistoricity and erasure I often observe and experience from white feminism.[11] It reminded me of all the times when I had been criticized for bringing up race in a discussion; the times I had been told that we were talking about gender, not race; and my frustration when I tried to explain that for so many people, gender and race are so intertwined as to be inextricable. I thought about all the people who probably wished I would just be quiet and wear the hat, march where and when they asked me to march, and applaud them for including me at all.

There is no need to whitewash the misdeeds of historical figures. Susan B. Anthony, Elizabeth Cady Stanton, and other white female abolitionists-turned-white-supremacists experienced sexism in the abolition movement. As a result, their feelings of abandonment led them to lash out at Black men who had been granted the right to vote. But Black women suffragists had even more reason to fear. Almost no one was speaking up for Black women's right to vote besides other Black women. Many prominent Black suffragists—Maria Stewart, Sojourner Truth, and Frances Harper among them—worked in both the abolition and the women's rights movements, but they grew tired of their marginalization within them.[12]

One example of this marginalization occurred during the Women's Suffrage March of 1913. Alice Paul, a march organizer, said that there must be "a white procession, or a Negro procession, or no procession at all."[13] The march was segregated, and Black suffragists were forced to march behind white suffragists to appease the Southern delegations. Ida B. Wells refused, joining the Illinois delegation and integrating the parade.

BLACK WOMEN AND THE CIVIL RIGHTS MOVEMENT

The Civil Rights Movement a few decades later was not much more hospitable to Black women. While this did not stop them from doing essential labor in the movement, it did create unique pressures, stressors, and obstacles to Black women assuming leadership positions and receiving credit for their work. This problem has existed since the beginning of civil rights activism. Anna Julia Cooper said that "the colored woman of today occupies ... a unique position in this country.... She is confronted by both a woman question and a race problem, and is as yet an unknown or unacknowledged factor in both."[14] This statement is as true today as when Cooper uttered it in 1892. Black women have always had to struggle simultaneously against multiple oppressions, and many of the most celebrated Black women of the movement experienced and spoke about constant sexism.

Whether objectification, discrimination, the withholding of leadership positions, or the erasure of parts of a legacy, sexism in the Civil Rights Movement took many forms. One example of this is Rosa Parks. People often think of her most famous moment of resistance—her refusal to give up her seat in the whites-only section of a bus in 1955 Montgomery, Alabama—as something she did because she was tired one day, rather than as a calculated act of civil disobedience. But indeed, it was one of many such intentional acts she performed throughout her life. While she may be known today for her choice not to give up her seat, Parks had already, by that time, worked for years as an anti-rape activist.[15]

Even after the bus incident, Rosa Parks did not receive offers of high-ranking leadership or strategic positions. Reflecting on her life of activism, Parks once said she felt like she had been forgotten: when she attended the historic march across the Edmund Pettus Bridge in Selma, Alabama, she recounted, the younger march attendees did not seem to recognize her or to be aware of her contributions to the movement.[16] That lack of recognition did not cause her to cease her labor for justice, but it perhaps circumscribed the scope of her impact.

Mrs. Parks was not the first Black woman to resist segregation in public transit, nor was she the first to receive media attention for it. Claudette Colvin, a fifteen-year-old Black girl, had done the same a few months before Parks. When reflecting on the moment when she had chosen to remain seated, Colvin said, "I felt like Sojourner Truth was pushing down on one shoulder and Harriet Tubman was pushing down on the other—saying 'Sit down, girl!' I was glued to my seat."[17] The NAACP considered taking Colvin's case national and using her story to challenge segregation laws across the country, but because she was a pregnant, unmarried teenager, it was decided that she did not embody the kind of "respectable womanhood" that would make her a sympathetic figure to the people whose minds the NAACP was trying to change. Instead, the NAACP organized action around Parks.

THE CONTRIBUTING ROLE OF PATRIARCHY

At least some of the sexism in the Civil Rights Movement can be attributed to the patriarchal structure of the church. Many of the most prominent civil rights organizations were birthed from the church, and church hierarchies carried over. In the church and in these organizations, Black women's labor was indispensable, even though they rarely held positions of authority.

Ella Baker was the first director of the Southern Christian Leadership Council (SCLC), founded in 1957. She was an effective community organizer; her gift for listening to the people she was serving and utilizing the assets they brought made her a successful and beloved leader. Even so, Baker was forced from her position as SCLC director in favor of men who were more deferential to hierarchical power structures and the organization's president,

Martin Luther King Jr. The SCLC continued to rely on Baker for her community organizing skills and contacts while stripping away her title and position and downplaying her centrality in the organization.

These slights did not cause Baker to leave the organization. Her split with the SCLC occurred because she found that it was not as responsive to the needs of the people as it should be. She wanted to move away from the centralized, hierarchal, male-dominated structures of the SCLC to a more egalitarian model. She wanted to empower young people to mobilize within their own communities to fight for justice in ways that were context specific and effective. These desires motivated her to help found the Student Nonviolent Coordinating Committee (SNCC) in 1960.[18]

SNCC members were responsible for many important civil rights actions. They led sit-ins, marches, voter registration drives, and freedom schools. The organization's members were present at virtually every major civil rights action in the 1960s, and they were often victims of violence at the hands of angry white people and the police. Baker's leadership and influence were visible in the organization's less hierarchical, more local structures. Women were able to lead and receive credit for their work with or without positional authority.

In spite of these foundational and structural frameworks, SNCC was not immune to the movement's patriarchy. Some women in the organization anonymously wrote a position paper titled "Women in the Movement," detailing their mistreatment and marginalization. They claimed they were often tasked with "menial and clerical" work instead of the field work they were capable of and wanted to do.[19] They also noted that men were still seen as the decision-makers and leaders. When asked what role women in SNCC should play, Stokely Carmichael, a prominent figure in SNCC who eventually began the Black Power movement, famously said, "The only position for women in SNCC is prone."[20] Whether joking or not, Stokely's quip captures the attitude many men held toward the women who were their fellow soldiers in the fight for equality.

THE SIGNIFICANCE OF INTERSECTIONALITY

While many Black women were personally frustrated with the sexism of the Civil Rights Movement and the racism of the women's equality movement, they also perceived this behavior as a strategic error. Black women have always known that our marginalization cannot be solved by focusing exclusively on racism or sexism. People with overlapping marginal identities experience a unique form of oppression. With that oppression comes an understanding that one cannot separate one's identities and fight the associated oppressions one at a time. This need to address injustice holistically framed the thinking and work of the Combahee River Collective, a group of mostly queer Black women feminists who worked to name and address the multiple dimensions of oppression and injustice they faced.

Formed in 1974, the Combahee River Collective took its name from a rescue mission conducted by Harriet Tubman.[21] The group comprised Black feminists from all over the country, many of whom had worked in various progressive organizations. Their shared belief, articulated in the Combahee River Collective Statement, was that racism, sexism, classism, homophobia, and all of the other types of oppression, while distinct, are overlapping and must be addressed holistically and simultaneously if true liberation is to occur. They believed that Black women would not experience true liberation as an auxiliary benefit to the women's rights movement or the Civil Rights Movement. They argued that Black women deserved to have their unique issues addressed as such. "Our politics initially sprang," they say in the statement, "from the shared belief that Black women are inherently valuable, and that our liberation is a necessity not as an adjunct to somebody else's but because of our need as human persons for autonomy."[22]

This statement is an explicit rejection of the idea that in working toward civil rights or women's rights generally, Black women would eventually become liberated by extension. While both movements benefited from the dedicated labor of Black women, each one failed to prioritize Black women's needs, often silencing them when they spoke up about such needs. The women of the Combahee River Collective refused to play into that dynamic. Instead, they centralized and prioritized the needs and experiences of Black women, affirming their intrinsic value. In doing so, the Combahee River Collective members did not abandon the fight against either racism or sexism, writing in their statement: "We struggle together with Black men against racism, while we also struggle with Black men about sexism."[23] In addition, because they realized that no movement valued Black women as much as they valued each other and themselves, they decided not to exert their precious energy trying to convince others that they deserved to be heard. They invested that energy in themselves.

As a Black woman, I have had to choose how to spend my energy in inhospitable places many times. In churches I have attended, leaders claimed to value the voices of women of color, but that seemed true only if they liked what those women had to say. A community of other Black women is what sustained me. Knowing I had a place where I would be understood without having to translate or explain, a place where I wouldn't be asked to leave a part of myself at the door, gave me the strength to keep working in the less inclusive spaces or to leave those spaces when that was the right choice.

The Combahee River Collective's focus on the lives of queer Black women exemplified intersectionality, a concept articulated and expanded by Dr. Kimberlé Crenshaw in 1989.[24] She created the metaphor to explain the fact that it is often impossible to determine whether the discrimination that Black women face is because of race or gender. Since it was first introduced, the concept of intersectionality has broadened to take other aspects of identity into account as well.

Intersectionality illustrates that people often have multiple identities that cause them to experience oppression or marginalization, and that in order to effectively address injustice, one must be aware of the experiences at the intersection of those identities. Black women should not have to put their race first in some places and their gender first in others. That is not how identity works. And it is not an effective way to tackle oppression. Black women, queer people of color, gender-nonconforming or nonbinary folks, and others who experience marginalization based on multiple identities should be able to show up as their full selves and be seen, heard, respected, and valued. This is especially true in justice-oriented spaces.

The model of movement building created by the Combahee River Collective provided an effective pattern for future justice movements to replicate. By addressing the overlapping oppression that Black women experience, especially if they are also queer, the Combahee River Collective set a precedent for Black female leadership and a focus on Black women's issues. The Black Lives Matter (BLM) movement is cut from this pattern. BLM is working incredibly hard to consider the conditions of the most oppressed within the Black community and to empower them to address their conditions effectively.

The Black Lives Matter movement sprang up when George Zimmerman, the man who murdered Trayvon Martin in 2012, was acquitted. Then, when Mike Brown was murdered in Ferguson, Missouri, in 2014, BLM activists and organizers from around the country traveled to support the protests. While the Black Lives Matter movement was started in response to the murders of cisgender Black men, the organizers work to center and celebrate the work done by Black women, nonbinary and gender-nonconforming Black folks, as well as queer Black folks. The co-founders, Alicia Garza, Patrisse Khan-Cullors, and Opal Tometi, are all Black women activists with long histories of advocating and agitating for equity and freedom in spaces defined by intersectional oppression.[25]

The phrase *intersectional feminism* has experienced a renaissance lately. It's become almost trendy to call oneself an intersectional feminist or to call someone out for their feminism not being intersectional enough. While this increased awareness has benefits, it also leads to a dilution of the principles of intersectionality and inclusivity. People can give lip service to the concept without actually understanding what it takes to pursue justice for the most marginalized.

Truly intersectional justice work is difficult. One must have an awareness of one's own identity, biases, and blind spots. One must be willing to center the people society pushes to the margins and trust them as experts on their own lives and on the most effective solutions to the issues that impact them. It requires humility and introspection. Though difficult, intersectionality is essential to effective justice work. Only when the most marginalized among us have been liberated can we all be truly free.

Cami Jones is a middle school English and US History teacher in Oakland, CA. Her goal is to equip her students to be critical, independent readers, thinkers, and writers, which means that she talks to them about justice and equity a lot. She loves getting lost in bookstores, museums, and redwood forests.

ENDNOTES

1   Erica Chenoweth and Jeremy Pressman, "This Is What We
     Learned by Counting the Women's Marches," *Washington
     Post*, February 7, 2017, www.washingtonpost.com/news/mon-
     key-cage/wp/2017/02/07/this-is-what-we-learned-by-count-
     ing-the-womens-marches/?noredirect=on&utm_term=.703ff-
     0d93e0a.

2   The Million Woman March took place October 25, 1997. Its
     purpose was to celebrate Black women and place at the cen-
     ter the social issues that impact them the most. Ashley Jones,
     "Million Woman March, 1997," Black Past, February 26, 2008,
     www.blackpast.org/aah/million-woman-march-1997.

3   Jamilah Lemieux, "Why I'm Skipping the Women's March
     on Washington [OPINION]," Colorlines, January 17, 2017,
     www.colorlines.com/articles/why-im-skipping-womens-march-
     washington-opinion.

4   Meredith Worthen, "The Women's Rights Movement and
     the Women of Seneca Falls," Biography, July 13, 2017, www.
     biography.com/news/seneca-falls-convention-leaders.

5   "Frederick Douglass," National Women's History Museum,
     accessed January 19, 2019, www.crusadeforthevote.org/doug-
     lass/.

6   U.S. Const. amend. XV, § 1.

7   Patricia G. Holland, "George Francis Train and the Woman
     Suffrage Movement, 1867–70," *Books at Iowa* 46 (April 1987),
     http://digital.lib.uiowa.edu/bai/holland.htm.

8   "Black Women & The Suffrage Movement: 1848–1923," Wes-
     leyan University, accessed January 19, 2019, www.wesleyan.
     edu/mlk/posters/suffrage.html#.

9   Ta-Nehisi Coates, "The Great Schism," *The Atlantic*, October
     18, 2011, www.theatlantic.com/national/archive/2011/10/the-
     great-schism/246640/.

10   "Remarks by Susan B. Anthony in the Circuit Court of the
       United States for the Northern District of New York 19 June
       1873," The Elizabeth Cady Stanton & Susan B. Anthony
       Papers Project, accessed January 19, 2019, http://ecssba.
       rutgers.edu/docs/sbatrial.html.

11   Anne Theriault, "The White Feminist Savior Complex,"
       Huffington Post, January 23, 2014; updated March 25,
       2014, https://www.huffingtonpost.com/anne-theriault-/
       the-white-feminist-savior_b_4629470.html.

12   "Sojourner Truth," History, October 29, 2009, last updated
       November 2, 2018, https://www.history.com/topics/black-his-
       tory/sojourner-truth; "Maria W. Stewart, an Early Abolition-
       ist," African American Registry, https://aaregistry.org/story/
       maria-w-stewart-an-early-abolitionist/; Melba Joyce Boyd,
       "Frances E.W. Harper & the Evolution of Radical Culture,"
       Solidarity, https://solidarity-us.org/atc/55/p2840/.

13   Michelle Bernard. "Despite the Tremendous Risk, African
       American Women Marched for Suffrage, Too," Washington
       Post, March 3, 2013, https://www.washingtonpost.com/blogs/
       she-the-people/wp/2013/03/03/despite-the-tremendous-risk-
       african-american-women-marched-for-suffrage-too/?.

14   Anna Julia Cooper, "The Status of Woman in America," in
       Words of Fire: An Anthology of African-American Feminist
       Thought, ed. Beverly Guy-Sheftall (New York: The New Press,
       1995), 45.

15   For more information: Danielle McGuire, At the Dark End of
       the Street: Black Women, Rape, and Resistance—A New Histo-
       ry of the Civil Rights Movement from Rosa Parks to the Rise of
       Black Power (New York: Alfred A. Knopf, 2010); and Rebecca
       Traister, Good and Mad: The Revolutionary Power of Women's
       Anger (New York: Simon & Schuster, 2018).

16   Jennifer Holladay, "Sexism in the Civil Rights Movement: A
       Discussion Guide," Teaching Tolerance, July 7, 2009, www.
       tolerance.org/magazine/sexism-in-the-civil-rights-movement-
       a-discussion-guide.

17   "Claudette Colvin Biography," Biography.com, April 1, 2014, last updated January 16, 2019, www.biography.com/people/ claudette-colvin-11378.

18   "The SCLC and the Birth of SNCC," Civil Rights Women Leaders of the Carolinas, April, 2013, https://ncwomenofcivilrights.wordpress.com/ella-baker/the-sclc-and-the-birth-of-sncc/.

19   "Student Nonviolent Coordinating Committee Position Paper: Women in the Movement," Veterans of the Civil Rights Movement: Women in the Movement, 2004, www.crmvet.org/ docs/snccfem.htm.

20   Sabina Peck, "'The Only Position for Women in SNCC Is Prone': Stokely Carmichael and the Perceived Patriarchy of Civil Rights Organisations in America," *History in the Making 1*, no. 1 (2012): 29-35, www.historyitm.org/index.php/hitm/ article/view/19/6.

21   For more information: Keeanga-Yamahtta Taylor, ed., *How We Get Free: Black Feminism and the Combahee River Collective* (Chicago: Haymarket Books, 2017).

22   Combahee River Collected Statement. The full statement can be found on Yale's American Studies program collection. https://americanstudies.yale.edu/sites/default/files/files/ Keyword%20Coalition_Readings.pdf.

23   Ibid.

24   For more information: Kimberlé Crenshaw's "The Urgency of Intersectionality," TEDWomen, October 2016, www.ted.com/ talks/kimberle_crenshaw_the_urgency_of_intersectionality.

25   For more information: Patrisse Khan-Cullors and asha bandele, *When They Call You a Terrorist: A Black Lives Matter Memoir* (New York: St. Martin's Press, 2018).

6

TWO CHRISTIANITIES

AMERICAN RELIGION IN BLACK AND WHITE

BY BRODERICK GREER

On any given Sunday during my teenage years, I could be found
in one of two places: a white evangelical Protestant church or
a historically black Protestant church, two designations Pew
Research uses when polling religion in the United States.[1]
While much of the hymnody, architectural style, and use of Bible
translations overlapped between the white and black Christianities,
unmentioned differences were rooted in their separate, but
intertwined, histories. For instance, the moderator of the black
Missionary Baptist district association to which my childhood
congregation belonged spoke out against the US invasion of Iraq
in a 2002 sermon that I vividly remember; the white evangelical
Protestant church I joined at age thirteen vigorously supported
use of force in the "War on Terror."[2] So while black and white
Christianities could easily recognize each other's liturgical
language—the love of God revealed in the death and resurrection of
Christ—the ways each extrapolated the doctrine were worlds apart.

One way in which the doctrinal differences are evident is in voting
patterns. As recently as the 2016 presidential election, black
and white Christians voted in wildly different ways. Republican
presidential nominee Donald Trump garnered 80 percent of the
white evangelical Protestant vote, while Democratic presidential
nominee Hillary Clinton earned 88 percent of the historically black

Protestant vote.[3] The division between white Roman Catholics and white mainline Protestants was almost nonexistent, as 48 percent and 49 percent respectively supported Donald Trump.[4] In the last four presidential elections, white Christians across the Roman Catholic–Protestant spectrum usually supported Republican candidates, while historically black Protestants overwhelmingly supported Democratic nominees.[5] These numbers also represent black and white Christians' views on war, torture, and other complex matters of social and moral significance. While diversity of opinion is nothing new to the Christian religion, the sharp points of departure between black and white Christians in the United States are notable for their breakdown according to race, not theology or doctrine.[6]

Attempts have been made throughout Christian history to distill the faith down to a single banner behind which all parties could march. In the church's first council, held in Jerusalem during the first century CE (Acts 15:1-35), Christians gathered to sort out questions about the role of Gentiles in the all-Jewish early Jesus movement—questions such as: "Should Gentile Christians be afforded the same standing in the church as its Jewish adherents?"

After heated discussions and robust concessions, the early Christians decided on a way forward that accommodated a number of constituencies, laying the groundwork for a theological framework spacious enough for various cultural tensions and what some considered taboos to coexist among the baptized people of God.[7] Baptism did not erase their differences, but they determined that their overarching unity in Christ allowed for diversity. Quandaries related to dietary norms, language, and other cultural touchstones came to be understood as worthy of a sort of ecclesiastical acceptance, and questions of whose Christianity would hold sway—the Jewish or the Gentile version—were resolved in a consensus that the people of God best inhabit the one body of Christ when they are allowed to retain their respective cultural, linguistic, and dietary norms.

This was decidedly *not* the approach taken as the Christian religion took shape in the United States. When Christianity came to North America, some European Christians made it their practice to propagate the religion among enslaved Africans.[8] But as enslaved black people began to convert to Christianity, white Christian enslavers quickly faced questions about the standing of black Christians in the nascent American society. Ultimately, after a revolt of enslaved Africans, white Christians decided that the social order must be retained. Thus, Christianity would reinforce white-supremacist ideals around lifelong enslavement. From that time through the Civil War, the majority of white Christians in the United States used Christianity as a tool of social control, highlighting Bible passages and interpretations that glorified enslavement and servitude.[9]

White lawmakers wrote, enacted, and enforced laws that placed strict parameters around the lives of black Christians. Part of these restrictions was to severely limit the rights of black Christians to organize their own churches, even though white Christians usually did not grant full church membership to black Christians. This led to the formation of historically black Protestant denominations like the African Methodist Episcopal Church, the Church of God in Christ, and the National Baptist Conventions, among others.

While white Christians justified the enslavement of African-descended peoples, African American Christians developed a method of biblical interpretation that called for the transformation of enslavement into liberation for people of African descent throughout the Atlantic World. This method of biblical interpretation and preaching read black people's experience of chattel enslavement into stories like the Israelites' deliverance from Egypt, creating an interpretive scaffolding that understood God as being on the side of the most vulnerable, not the most powerful. Sometimes this method led to proactive physical resistance to enslavement. Other times it led to a quiet, internal resistance that served as a motivating impetus for enslaved black people to simply survive the grueling conditions of life as property of white people. Both allowed African-descended Christians a semblance of dignity not legally or socially afforded them by the majority of white Christian Americans.

The more African Americans converted to Christianity, the more the US government cracked down on their ability to lawfully assemble because of white Christian enslavers' nervousness about revolts in the style of Nat Turner's Rebellion.* Revolts could upend a social order that was advantageous to white Americans' generations-long accrual of wealth, land, people, and power. In pulpits and Sunday schools, white clergymen promoted biblical interpretations that reinforced a white Christian–supremacist social order while black Christians developed music, sermons, and a "sanctified imagination" in which "All of God's children got shoes"[10] and one's "trust in the Lord" would lead to "treat[ing] everybody right."[11] This development of two parallel Christianities is a major feature of what Bishop William Barber calls "slaveholder religion" and "the freedom church."[12] Bishop Barber's distinction between the two Christianities is a helpful reference point in regard to race and Christianity, especially amid an effort to minimize the differences between the two or maintain the idea that Christianity in the United States is a monolithic enterprise.[13]

For that very reason, white American religious language about "unity in Christ" or being "one in the gospel" is not only misleading, but harmful. At best, language that centers white and black Christian unity is aspirational, since the legacy of white-imposed ecclesial segregation remains with us to this day. While many quote the Rev. Dr. Martin Luther King Jr. saying that 11:00 a.m. on Sunday is "one of the most segregated hours" in US life, few offer an explanation of why this is so.[14] In their failure to recall the disease itself, they offer verbal treatment to the symptoms of ongoing social and religious fractures rooted in white supremacy. As alluded to earlier, the African Methodist Episcopal Church, the National (Black) Baptist Conventions, and other historically black

---

*Nat Turner led a slave rebellion in 1831, killing more than fifty white people. Nat Turner and fifty-five other slaves were executed for their participation.

Protestant traditions are historically black because the same white ministers who preached the gospel of Jesus Christ to black people did not accept or assume the full humanity of black people.

THE PROBLEM WITH RECONCILIATION

This deep-seated amnesia of history causes some white Christians to use reconciliation language while not realizing that one cannot reconcile something that was never itself conciliatory. In recent years, especially in the wake of highly publicized police shootings of black people,[15] the election of a self-proclaimed white "nationalist" president,[16] and the rise of hate crimes perpetrated by white supremacists,[17] some white Christians have made it their prerogative to interrogate and root out white supremacy in white American Christianity. While the efforts are noble, they can also end up doing more harm than good if not rooted in the socio-historical context discussed thus far in this chapter.

One majority-white Christian denomination deeply interested in what they call "racial reconciliation" is the Southern Baptist Convention, the largest Protestant denomination in the United States. At its 1995 annual convention in Atlanta, Georgia, the Southern Baptist Convention passed a resolution on racial reconciliation to mark the 150th anniversary of the denomination's founding, which resulted from nineteenth-century theological and political disputes about the enslavement of black people.[18] Twenty-two years later, at its 2017 annual convention in Phoenix, Arizona, the denomination passed a resolution condemning the alt-right and "decry[ing] every form of racism."[19] This resolution was only passed, however, after an earlier resolution failed because of what the *New York Times* called "harsh wording."[20]

The Rev. Dwight McKissic, founder and senior pastor of Cornerstone Baptist Church in Arlington, Texas, was the convention messenger who proposed the initial version of the resolution in Phoenix. I grew up in Fort Worth, Texas, just twenty minutes away from Pastor McKissic's church, and attended high school with many of his parishioners. As an adolescent attending a black Missionary Baptist Church that belonged to a historically black Baptist denomination, I assumed that Cornerstone was a member of the same. Little did I know that Cornerstone not only belongs to the Southern Baptist Convention—85 percent of which is white—but that the Convention generously funded the church's founding.[21] The original "harsh wording" the 2017 convention messengers rejected included the characterization of white nationalism and the so-called "alt-right" as a "toxic menace."[22] For a denomination that frequently uses the term "racial reconciliation," its reluctance to enthusiastically endorse this terminology in McKissic's initial resolution is curious.

Any attempt at forging "racial reconciliation" without a robust articulation of how contemporary white Americans continue to benefit from violent economic, social, political, and theological wrongs done in the name of whiteness is for naught. A white denomination may pass resolutions apologizing for its racist past, plant congregations that target communities of color for membership, and elect clergy of color to its highest ranks, but if that denomination cannot truly reckon with its present participation in white supremacy, it will sabotage its own well-intentioned efforts.

Additionally, talk of "racial reconciliation" without proper critical analyses of power, race, and gender inequities can lead to the assimilation of black people in predominantly white Christian settings. Dr. Chanequa Walker-Barnes has said, "A church can be multiracial yet culturally homogenous because all power and influence in the congregation is held by members of the same cultural group."[23] The same can apply to parachurch organizations, media ministries, and other expressions of white Christian hegemony in which assimilation to whiteness is valued over black Christians' maintaining of liturgical language, imagery, and iconography rooted in black American Christianity.

REDEFINING LIBERATION

It is unwise for us to rush toward multiculturalism as the only way to dismantle and replace a white-supremacist Christian framework. Christians conscious of the power and sway of whiteness must always guard against the impulse toward whiteness and its allergy to particularity. To live within a white Christian supremacist paradigm is to understand whiteness—its idioms, biases, and assumptions—as the default; hence the proclivity of some to say, "All lives matter" when they hear another say, "Black lives matter." For those who say "all lives matter," 'all' includes white, black, and every other color; however, they fail to recognize that specific manifestations of white supremacy call for specific solutions and that black lives in particular are worthy of specific attention and protection. This became most apparent to me when I visited my great-grandfather's grave in East Texas a few years ago.

After an almost four-hour drive, I finally found the church cemetery in which my mother's grandfather and uncle are buried. After the dust from the red clay roads settled, I left my car and walked over to the church bell tower, where I was stunned to find the following words: "Founded 1865." In all my years of hearing stories of my maternal grandmother playing the piano for services at that particular church and of relatives being buried on its lush green land for the better part of a century, I had never once heard about the year of the church's founding. This is significant because, while enslaved black people in other parts of the United States were emancipated on January 1, 1863, enslaved black people in my home state of Texas were not emancipated until June 19, 1865, meaning that 1865 was the first year in American history in which all African Americans could formally and legally begin founding their own houses of worship and other private organizations.

On the journey home, all I could think about was what that first worship service in that rural black church must have been like: the hymns they sang, the sermon they heard, the prayers they prayed, and the stories they told. In my sanctified imagination, I hear, echoing down through time from the early years of this congregation, feet stomping on the second and fourth beats, conveying a divine immediacy in the rhythm of my ancestors. I see in my mind's eye people young and old laboring together over weeks to construct their first sanctuary. I smell the frequent fresh, home-cooked feasts prepared by hands irreversibly deformed by lifetimes of dehumanizing enslavement. And I see, some years later, my maternal grandmother and her four siblings standing at their father's graveside as the minister of this church scatters dust on his wooden coffin. Finally, I hear the church bell toll: announcing, over the years, weddings, burials, and countless Sunday calls to prayer for those tending nearby land.

In the evolution of black Christianities in the United States, it is difficult to divorce black embodiment from one's experience of God. My maternal grandmother, like many black people born in the first half of the twentieth century, was raised close to the land. Her family planted and harvested peaches, sorghum, and watermelons and raised pigs and cows. This may very well explain why so many of the elders in my black childhood church would, when referring to the Divine, say, "My God owns the cattle of a thousand hills." For my grandmother, for black people of her generation, and for their ancestors in black Christian faith, one's connection to the land was inseparable from how one experienced God as a generous and loving provider.

Deep in the DNA of the black Christianity in which I was reared is the question my mother often confronted me with: "If white people claim to be Christians, how are they capable of being racist?" My mother's question is not only a fair interrogation of whiteness, but a natural outgrowth of the theodicy created by the presence of whiteness in the lives of black people. On one hand, her question assumes that at the center of any expression of Christianity is the person of Jesus Christ, whose life, death, and resurrection are a divine critique of xenophobia, state violence, and homogenous narratives. On the other hand, my mother's question contests deceptive interpretations of Christianity that not only have nothing useful to say about pressing social ills, but ignore their participation in perpetuating white supremacy, chattel enslavement that later gave rise to the Industrial Revolution and unrestrained capitalism, and ongoing racial terror. While I do not have a particularly tidy answer to my mother's lifelong question, I do think her question deserves serious contemplation. My mother's question acknowledges that while white and black Christianities might have similar vocabularies, the words the two share have disparate definitions.

This leads me to wonder: If my ancestral church was not founded until 1865—at the end of the era of enslavement—what new dimensions of liberation are waiting for our attention in this day? While I may not be attuned to what those are, we can cultivate our hearts so as to prepare ourselves for what is to come, and we can do so in two ways: by finding new heroes, and by believing people the first time they show you who they are.

FINDING NEW HEROES

In story after story, Jesus places at the center the least likely characters—those society places at the margins. In Matthew's Gospel, to the chagrin of his disciples, Jesus gathers despised children to himself and blesses them (19:13-15), crossing the boundaries of ancient assumptions that children were not fully human. In Mark's Gospel, Jesus is approached by a Syrophoenician woman requesting that he heal her daughter. Instead of focusing on Jesus' generosity toward the woman, the narrator emphasizes how the woman's faithful persistence resulted in her daughter's recovery (7:24-29). In Luke's Gospel, just after condemning religious and political leaders who live lavish lives on the backs of widows, Jesus commends the generosity of an impoverished widow (20:45—21:4). And in John's Gospel, Jesus rides into Jerusalem on a young donkey, not a steed (12:12-19), illustrating that when God runs the world, humility—not power—will have final say in the direction of our common future. With all these accounts and more readily available to us in Scripture, it is past time for Christians to tell, embody, and anticipate counterintuitive stories that echo the counterintuitive God who makes the last first and the first last. In our proclamation of the good news of Jesus, his way of telling and enacting stories must become ours.

"WHEN PEOPLE SHOW YOU WHO THEY ARE, BELIEVE THEM THE FIRST TIME."

Dr. Maya Angelou made this comment to Oprah Winfrey in an interview regarding romantic relationships.[24] Dr. Angelou's remark is sagacious insofar as it also applies more broadly to human trauma and experience. For centuries, black people have expressed grievance after grievance, prompting replies from white counterparts like, "That just sounds too cruel to be true." When black people's experiences of white supremacy are not taken seriously and acted upon by white people, white people invalidate black people's lived reality. Treating black people's experiences as a piece of interpersonal trivia is actually a shield for white Christians against what German Catholic theologian Johannes Baptist Metz has called "dangerous memory": that is, an "unforgetting" that claims that the suffering, crucifixion, and resurrection of Jesus Christ should cause us to bring to an end suffering among the world's most oppressed populations.[25]

A dimension of striving to believe people the first time is trusting their account of the horrors they've experienced in the face of profound dehumanization. It means resisting the urge to debate someone's experience and, instead, saying, "I see you. I hear you. Your truth is now at home inside of me." The dangerous memories of the transatlantic slave trade, chattel enslavement, the Jim and Jane Crow era, and present-day injustice hold the potential to transform a world propped up by structural anti-blackness and white supremacy. Embedded in all of that is the expectation that

God will actively, joyfully intervene in the middle of history to liberate God's people from the hands of God's enemies—namely, those abusing people and power.

A 2015 graduate of Virginia Theological Seminary, the Rev. Canon Broderick Greer is Canon Precentor at Saint John's Cathedral in Denver, Colorado where he oversees liturgy and young adult ministry. Broderick speaks on matters related to history, black and queer theology, and racial justice. His work has appeared in The Guardian, Teen Vogue, On Being, *and the* Washington Post.

ENDNOTES

1   Pew Research Center, "Appendix B: Classification of Protestant Denominations," America's Changing Religious Landscape, May 12, 2015, www.pewforum.org/2015/05/12/appendix-b-classification-of-protestant-denominations/.

2   Religion News Service, "Religious Groups Issue Statements on War with Iraq," Pew Religious Center, March 19, 2003, www.pewforum.org/2003/03/19/publicationpage-aspxid616/.

3   Ryan P. Burge, "The 2016 Religious Vote (for More Groups Than You Thought Possible)," Religion in Public, March 10, 2017, https://religioninpublic.blog/2017/03/10/the-2016-religious-vote-for-more-groups-than-you-thought-possible/.

4   Daniel Cox and Robert P. Jones, "The 2016 Religion Vote," Public Religion Research Institute, October 27, 2016, www.prri.org/spotlight/religion-vote-2016/.

5   "How Groups Voted," Roper Center for Public Opinion Research, https://ropercenter.cornell.edu/data-highlights/elections-and-presidents/how-groups-voted.

6   Theology does not occur in a vacuum, for it is always the way we speak about God from our own cultures, biases, and assumptions.

7   This is in no way a subscription to views of early Christianities that place the first-century church as an ideal or a model to elevate. Early Christianities, just like Christianities of our own time, had their own unique challenges, strengths, and complexities.

8   Katharine Gerbner, *Christian Slavery: Conversion and Race in the Protestant Atlantic World* (Philadelphia: University of Pennsylvania Press, 2018).

9   This is an "apples and oranges" situation because the racialized chattel enslavement of the sixteenth to nineteenth centuries was different from the class-based indentured servitude of the ancient Roman world.

10   The Charioteers, "All God's Chillun Got Shoes," Le Gospel 1939–1952 Disc 1 (video, 3:08), https://www.youtube.com/watch?v=b2pjdAFLsWw.

11   Charles Taylor, "I Will Trust in the Lord" (video, 2:21), www.youtube.com/watch?v=maF3IULw81Q.

12   Ken Camp, "Author Contrasts Slaveholder Religion and the Freedom Church," Baptist Standard, November 19, 2018, www.baptiststandard.com/news/texas/author-con-trasts-slaveholder-religion-and-the-freedom-church/.

13   As with any binary-based categorization, there are always exceptions. A glaring exception to white "slaveholder religion" is the small, but conscientious, number of white Christians who worked for the abolition of enslavement, for an end to Jim/Jane Crow laws, and for the economic, social, and political equity due the descendants of the 4 million Africans enslaved and brought to what is now the United States. While their contribution to the common good is notable, they are still exceptions to the rule, not the rule itself. Also, within various majority-white Christian denominations there are usually a number of black adherents and adherents of color. The presence, however, of black adherents in a majority-white denomination does not eliminate a given denomination's history of excluding and exploiting black Americans.

14   "The Most Segregated Hour in America – Martin Luther King Jr." (interview clip), *Meet the Press*, April 17, 1960, www.youtube.com/watch?v=1q881g1L_d8.

15   Jasmine C. Lee and Haeyoun Park, "15 Black Lives Ended in Confrontations with Police. 3 Officers Convicted," *New York Times*, updated October 5, 2018, www.nytimes.com/interac-tive/2017/05/17/us/black-deaths-police.html.

16   Aaron Blake, "Trump's Embrace of a Fraught Term—'Nationalist'—Could Cement a Dangerous Racial Divide," *Washington Post*, October 23, 2018, www.washingtonpost.com/politics/2018/10/23/trumps-embrace-fraught-term-nationalist-could-cement-dangerous-racial-divide/?noredi-rect=on&utm_term=.5d347781e3cd.

17   John Eligon, "Hate Crimes Increase for the Third Consecutive Year, F.B.I. Reports," *New York Times*, November 13, 2018, www.nytimes.com/2018/11/13/us/hate-crimes-fbi-2017.html.

18   "Resolution on Racial Reconciliation on the 150th Anniversary of the Southern Baptist Convention," Southern Baptist Convention (1995), www.sbc.net/resolutions/899/resolution-on-racial-reconciliation-on-the-150th-anniversary-of-the-southern-baptist-convention.

19   "On the Anti-Gospel of Alt-Right White Supremacy," Southern Baptist Convention (2017), www.sbc.net/resolutions/2283/on-the-antigospel-of-altright-white-supremacy.

20   Jacey Fortin, "In Quick Reversal, Southern Baptists Denounce White Nationalists," *New York Times,* June 15, 2017, www.nytimes.com/2017/06/15/us/southern-baptist-convention-alt-right-resolution.html.

21   William Dwight McKissic Sr., "I'm a Black Pastor. Here's Why I'm Staying in the Southern Baptist Convention," *Washington Post*, August 2, 2017, www.washingtonpost.com/news/acts-of-faith/wp/2017/08/02/im-a-black-pastor-heres-why-im-staying-in-the-southern-baptist-convention/?utm_term=.714aaf72c985.

22   Dwight McKissic, "Resolution for the 2017 SBC Annual Meeting – Condemning the Alt-Right & White Nationalism," SBC Voices, May 28, 2017, https://sbcvoices.com/resolution-for-the-2017-sbc-annual-meeting-condemning-the-alt-right-white-nationalism/.

23   Chanequa Walker-Barnes, "Why Multicultural Churches Fail – Part One," Bearings Online, May 31, 2018, https://collegevilleinstitute.org/bearings/why-multicultural-churches-fail/.

24   "When People Show You Who They Are, Believe Them," Oprah's Life Class (video clip, 3:58), episode aired October 26, 2011, OWN TV, www.oprah.com/oprahs-lifeclass/when-people-show-you-who-they-are-believe-them-video.

25   Michael Kirwan, "Awakening Dangerous Memories," *The Way* 47, no. 4 (October 2008): 25–36, www.theway.org.uk/Back/474Kirwan.PDF.

7

A NEW HEAVEN AND A NEW EARTH

THE PROBLEM WITH RACIAL RECONCILIATION

BY LENNY DUNCAN

It's safe to say that Christianity calls for a just future. But what does a just future look like? For Christians, how you answer will depend on your social location in relation to the gospel of Jesus Christ. A related, and perhaps more important, question is this: How do we live out the gospel in this generation, in this time, in this place?

We argue whether or not the immigrant is welcome in our land. We debate whether or not it's justifiable for black bodies to be killed by police. We have watched as children die on our borders during the Christmas season. We are more ready than ever to cry foul when our institution is called systemically racist. We stand among the tattered threads of humanity and refuse to hear their cries. As we look across the landscape of the American church in the twenty-first century, no matter where we find ourselves we have to account for not only a bloody past, but also a bloody present, in which the practice of crucifying people of color like me still happens on the streets of this country.

So I ask: How do we work together as the church toward a just and holy future?

FACING THE HARD TRUTHS

The days of weak theological statements, or public letters signed by clergy and laity, in protest or concern about societal injustices have passed. While well intended, such efforts are, at best, an academic exercise in racial equity and justice and, at worst, counterproductive feel-good devices that placate us and keep us from taking action in our own lives and communities. We're past that.

We need to have a final reckoning with radical evil and the forces that defy God. We need to name and claim them. White supremacy is a systemic force in this world that defies God. It is an insidious system that does not require you or anyone you know to be actively racist. Its narrative, devices, and levers of power have been baked into the very bones of this country and the church. It doesn't matter whether you benefit from it passively or reinforce it unconsciously through your own actions. Everyone who claims the name Christian is complicit in its continued existence, and we have to work as the whole body of Christ to deconstruct and dismantle it. If one wants to make the claim that "all are welcome," one has to critique the power structures that exist within the body of Christ.

But critique is not an end in itself. The whole point of critique is to take stock of what's happening so you can grow toward the future: a future full of possibility and the Holy Spirit; a future that mirrors the unveiling, the apocalypse, the revelation of the kin-dom of God. I say "kin-dom" because a kingdom implies a ruler or leader. We, on the other hand, are building a beloved, egalitarian community of kinfolk—the family of Christ. And like in other major institutions, it'll often be led by women and people of color and LGBTQIA folks.

If you have been along for most or all of this study on race, you have already explored some of the real hurt, pain, and historical trauma perpetrated on my ancestors, perhaps by some of yours. You already know some of the ugliest points of the intersection between church and race. This is an uncomfortable place, and I acknowledge that. I invite you to stay in the place of uncertainty, pain, and lament. Feel it—don't try to fix it. There seems to be a white Protestant obsession with running to reconciliation. From your vantage point now, it would be a welcome retreat, a respite from the realities of white supremacy and systemic oppression in this country. I'll be so bold as to remind you that I get no such break. I don't get to opt out or walk away. I don't get to decide that this is too hard and throw in the towel. I don't get to allow my reticence to see the suffering of others, or my anger at the suggestion that I might play a part in it, to be an excuse for a way out. Whether you choose to ignore or actively take part in dismantling racism in your community, I still suffer under it. Every day.

That doesn't mean we don't have a future. We are a people of hope. Built into the very DNA of the church—in every living, breathing cell of the body of Christ—is hope. It is the hope of the tomb that was found empty, bereft of life but also bereft of death! Hope is the fulcrum of all life in the universe. It is from this place of hope that we begin to explore a just and equitable future.

DOING THE HARD WORK

I believe the only hope for mainline Christianity is to dismantle white supremacy—first in our pews and then in our communities. This is the call of discipleship. With the rise of xenophobia, racial violence, and nationalism in the United States, it's hard to deny the roots of the real hurt people of color experience in the system of white supremacy. White supremacy is antithetical to the gospel. White supremacy is a power that defies God. To name a thing *radical evil* is dangerous work. To actively push back against it? Well, that's enough to get you crucified. This kind of work requires a deep level of commitment, and the road ahead will be hard. Full stop.

It doesn't get easier. In fact, it is my experience that an anti-racist walk with Christ can be at times overwhelmingly exhausting. But Christianity has never been a safe path; it has always been fraught with self-sacrifice and the pouring out of one's life for others.

The church's history is full of examples. The Rev. Dr. Martin Luther King Jr. lived a life of self-sacrifice and honor. But he received the "prophet's reward" (Matthew 10:41) at the end of his ministry. In America that means a violent end, usually a bullet. Or look at the organizers from the Ferguson, Missouri, uprising in 2014. Many have died under mysterious circumstances or by suicide.[1] That's because freedom isn't free. It is bought and paid for by the lives of those who fight for something they may never live to see the results of.

Hear this, Church: You are the fragrant offering on the altar of oppression. You are the grace wafting up to a God who is ready to empower you for this work. You are the fire that falls down on the church of every generation. You are the embodiment of the Holy Spirit. You can be the gospel.

If we want to have a just and equitable future, we have to actually look to the church's past and the radical roots of Scripture. The narrative arc of Scripture is the story of a loving God who liberates oppressed people throughout human history. God's activity, intervention, and interaction in the world have scattered grace, mercy, and liberation across the globe. This is our inheritance as people of God—this sacred story of liberation—and it's also our blueprint for moving forward.

THE FUTURE AND THE CHURCH

I want to present to you a simple idea, but one that appears over and over in Scripture: God expresses God's grace in diversity.

At the tower of Babel, we gather as one people. After the flood narrative, humanity had assembled into one culture with one language. What happens? We try to make ourselves like God; we use our best thinking and ability to "climb to the heavens." This is a story of the human capacity to seek ultimate power, and this attempt is facilitated by a homogenous society. It is propped up by the often-repeated dream of one united world. How does a loving God save us from ourselves? God's saving action is to give us diversity of culture, language, location, and peoplehood.

In Acts 2, when the once fearful disciples are gathered waiting for the Advocate to come, what happens? They are suddenly filled with God's power and might, and they declare God's saving actions in the world. The Holy Spirit flows from them as from overfilled cups. Holy fire escapes their every pore. What does that sound like in the world? It sounds like the hundreds of diverse languages and dialects that are within earshot on this festival day. It sounds like a symphony of the human experience! It sounds like hundreds of tongues and falls on the ears of an array of hearers. God declares the inauguration of the church in diversity.

Finally, in Revelation, at the end of the narrative, our loving and gracious God calls all peoples, all tribes, all nations to a new heaven and a new earth, established right where we are sitting right now— on this planet! All the disparate threads of humanity are finally woven into one inclusive tapestry. The very stones of creation shout the name of Jesus this day. Creation shouts that name in thousands of dialects. God's expression of love, grace, and salvation is diversity.

So, I want to talk to you about what it means to be co-creators of a new heaven and a new earth. As the church, you have been called to the work of the very heavens! You are blessed beyond understanding because you sit on the precipice of something incredible. You are the foundation, the sure ground, the very stage upon which grace will act—will bring life out of death and love out of hate in echoes of the resurrection of Christ. You are sitting where the breach will be repaired. You are the tools that the Great Sculptor will use to chip away at hatred, prejudice, economic inequality, and all the rest of the bundled demons in the legion called systemic racism. You have been handcrafted, selected, and prepared from the beginning of the cosmos for this time and place; called to help create a new and stunning vision. You have been invited into a new "genesis" through the "revelations" you have encountered together in this time spent studying the raw, screaming face of white supremacy.

A new and just future must take seriously not only repentance, but even more importantly, restoration. There must be a restoration to human order, and we as the church can take the lead. A just future means that we are unafraid to take to the streets in solidarity with #BlackLivesMatter or the Poor People's Campaign. A just future means ending cash bail in your county. A just future means that you take a look at your imagery of Jesus and ask yourself why a man from the Middle East looks so white. But more importantly, it's your time to stop making excuses for why you aren't active in the battle for the soul of this country. The real question you must reflect upon is: What is the church even worth in the twenty-first century if it doesn't respond to the continued oppression of black and brown bodies in the United States? We would be a whitewashed tomb with no witness to bear to the saints who follow us into this tradition, this path of grace.

We have to cover just a little more ground, y'all. Just a little further. Because Jesus wants more. Just a little bit more.

What might a new heaven and a new earth, free of systemic racism and oppression, look like? I can't imagine, to be honest. I can't imagine a world where my father would have been truly able to love me because he wasn't so beaten down by the world. I can't imagine a world in which the Philadelphia school system would have noticed that he couldn't read before high school, rather than ignoring him to such an extent that they weren't aware. I can't image a world where I wasn't called "nigger" by friends growing up as a last resort in a petty schoolyard squabble. A world where I wasn't targeted for minor marijuana charges as a teen and my life thrown into chaos. A world where I don't grip the steering wheel of my car wondering whenever I get pulled over whether my life is ending. My existence has been colored by the hues of my people's blood my entire life, my father's life, and his father's life. But I can tell you what I think the work of achieving this new heaven and earth may look like.

We have to start by looking at our theology—specifically, the way in which we tell God's story with a "hermeneutic of suspicion"—that is, through an interpretive lens that leads us to think critically and ask hard and honest questions. We have to be willing to take millennia-old thoughts about God's interaction with our world and make wholesale changes if necessary. I mean really throw the whole Christian experiment in a pot and cook it down to its very essence. Let it simmer until all we are left with is the Apostles' Creed. Before we add another ingredient, we have to look around the table and see who is seated with us. We have to ask: Who is not represented here, and why?

We have to start almost from scratch, like the first apostles did. In Matthew 15:21-28, Jesus models what this might look like:

> Jesus left that place and went away to the district of Tyre and Sidon. Just then a Canaanite woman from that region came out and started shouting, "Have mercy on me, Lord, Son of David; my daughter is tormented by a demon." But he did not answer her at all. And his disciples came and urged him, saying, "Send her away, for she keeps shouting after us." He answered, "I was sent only to the lost sheep of the house of Israel." But she came and knelt before him, saying, "Lord, help me." He answered, "It is not fair to take the children's food and throw it to the dogs." She said, "Yes, Lord, yet even the dogs eat the crumbs that fall from their masters' table." Then Jesus answered her, "Woman, great is your faith! Let it be done for you as you wish." And her daughter was healed instantly.

Jesus denies the woman who seeks him out, who comes to him when he is trying to withdraw from the world. This is a difficult story to try to reconcile with the overall narrative of the gospel. Why would Jesus do this? How do we fit this episode into Jesus being the Son of God and the Savior of the world? Why would the writer of Matthew even leave this story in? We know Jesus did much more than what is recorded in the Gospels, so why record this? Gospel writers went to great lengths to prove that Jesus is the Messiah, yet this story stands out in its seemingly callous depiction of Jesus.

I believe that other than the scene in the Garden of Gethsemane, this is Jesus' most human moment. It is in this moment that we see him as a person embedded in a culture that has told him he is far superior to the people of Tyre and Sidon; that as a Jewish person, he is better than the Canaanites, whom his own people slaughtered centuries back for control of the promised land; that he is of the chosen people, and that he has come only for the chosen people. This is a shocking message, the kind one would expect from a nationalist, not the Son of God.

But then Jesus changes his mind. He admits he was wrong. He changes his actions.

What if the church could be like Jesus in this way, using this scripture as a model? What if the church just accepted that it has been wrong, that what it has been enculturated with and taught to believe is flawed, and that the ministry of the church might in fact be much bigger than we have envisioned? The Canaanite woman represents the four hundred years of suffering of indigenous brown and black bodies on this continent. We have been screaming out, "Have mercy on us, Church! Our children, our siblings are tormented by a demon!"

The American church has told us through its actions that the people who truly deserve its love are the children of Europe. And the progressive church movement is just as guilty—they have become like the "white moderate" in Rev. Dr. King's "Letter from a Birmingham City Jail": "more devoted to order than to justice."[2] Nothing is more disappointing than stepping into a supposedly anti-racist and egalitarian space only to discover a recreation of the same system of empire one was hoping to escape.

But like Jesus in this text, we can realize our error, our pride, our mistake. We can declare at the table of grace that more than just crumbs are meant for all people. We could declare a commitment to black and brown people in progressive churches and other spaces. A new heaven and a new earth could start there. But the end result of such a vison would be much larger.

If I were to dream, I would say it would look like every church in America hitting the streets on the anniversary of Trayvon Martin's death—everyone wearing hoodies, drinking iced tea, and passing out Skittles to police.

A new heaven and a new earth might mean emptying out all the church savings and investment accounts and setting up a cash bail fund for those who can't afford it, who could never afford it, who are living lives designed to never be able to make bail.

A new heaven and a new earth might mean that we start local farms and end food deserts in our urban areas.

A new heaven and a new earth might mean the leadership of your church and at least 75 percent of the congregation doing a three-day anti-racism training every three years because you understand that this is not a one-and-done thing.

A new heaven a new earth might mean that if your church building was constructed by slave labor, you track down the descendants of those people and pay them the wages they are owed with interest, even if that means closing the doors of your church.

A new heaven and a new earth might mean that you and the entire congregation spend a week attending Immigration and Customs Enforcement (ICE) hearings as holy witnesses and let the judge know that the eyes of the church of God are upon them and that this macabre human tragedy is not going unnoticed.

A new heaven and a new earth might mean that we no longer place straight white men at the center of the theology studied in our seminaries; that we offer black, Latinx, indigenous, and Asian theologians' writings *as central texts*—not as add-ons or extra reading, which is often the case in even the most progressive seminary spaces.

A new heaven and a new earth might mean that we take into account that although we may be an "affirming" church, the average life span for a black trans woman in this country is thirty-five years. Despite the pivotal role played by trans women of color such as Marsha P. Johnson and Sylvia Rivera in establishing the LGBTQIA rights movement, transgender violence continues today as the modern form of lynching. In a new heaven and a new earth, you'd be holding Good Friday services at the scene of Johnson's lynching, weeping at the foot of the cross with Mary. You'd know that this is a horror being perpetrated on the most vulnerable.

In a new heaven and a new earth, you would know that if you don't understand the history of lynching in America, then you don't understand the crucifixion of Jesus Christ. Full stop.

In a new heaven and a new earth, you would understand that one does not need documents to be a citizen of God's kin-dom; that no one's inherent worth is based on the imaginary lines drawn on maps.

We can catch glimpses of this just and equitable world, but we will never fully know what it will be like until it arrives. I can't imagine a world where I would have true freedom. I have only seen hints of it in Scripture. It is like the wind across my face: I know of its presence, but have yet to capture it, hold it, or make it stay.

Yet we worship a God with power to make the unknowable, the unthinkable, the things that lie just beyond the edges of our imagination real. Incarnate. Enfleshed. It is that hope, that resurrection promise, that keeps me going every day. My sincere prayer is that it's enough to invite you into this work, into a lifetime of struggle and solidarity, into a lifetime of discipleship and self-sacrifice.

I honor the work you have done through this course to even contemplate pouring your life out for people you may never meet. I love you. You are beloved and will receive power from on high. I know that you are not alone, because I have never been alone. Amen.

Lenny Duncan is pastor of Jehu's Table, a church in the heart of Brooklyn. Formerly incarcerated, formerly homeless, and formerly unchurched, Duncan is now a sought-after speaker and writer on topics of racial justice and the role of the church in the twenty-first century. His documentary film, Do Black Churches Matter in the ELCA, *was released in 2017. His first book* Dear Church: A Love Letter from a Black Preacher to the Whitest Denomination in the US, *was published in July 2019 by Fortress Press.*

ENDNOTES

1   Jason Johnson, "Ferguson, Mo, Activists Are Dying and It's
     Time To Ask Questions," *The Root*, May 5, 2017, accessed
     March 7, 2019, https://www.theroot.com/ferguson-activists-
     are-dying-and-it-s-time-to-ask-quest-1794955900.

2   Martin Luther King Jr., "Letter from Birmingham Jail"
     (August 1963), 3, https://web.cn.edu/kwheeler/documents/
     Letter_Birmingham_Jail.pdf.

MORE RESOURCES ON RACE

BOOKS

Adichie, Chimamanda Ngozi. *We Should All Be Feminists*. New York: Anchor, 2015.

Baffes, Melanie, ed. *Text and Context: Vernacular Approaches to the Bible in Global Christianity*. Eugene, OR: Pickwick Publications, 2018.

Boesak, Allan Aubrey, and Curtiss Paul DeYoung. *Radical Reconciliation: Beyond Political Pietism and Christian Quietism*. Maryknoll, NY: Orbis, 2012.

Boyd, Drick. *White Allies in the Struggle for Racial Justice*. Maryknoll, NY: Orbis, 2015.

Carruthers, Charlene A. *Unapologetic: A Black, Queer, and Feminist Mandate for Radical Movements*. Boston: Beacon, 2018.

Cooper, Brittany. *Eloquent Rage: A Black Feminist Discovers Her Superpower*. New York: St. Martin's Press, 2018.

Deloria, Jr., Vine. *God is Red: A Native View of Religion*. New York: Putnam, 1973.

Moxnes, Halvor. *A Short History of the New Testament*. London: I.B. Tauris, 2014.

Nerburn, Kent. *Neither Wolf Nor Dog: On Forgotten Roads With An Indian Elder*. Novato, CA: New World Library, 1994.

Räisänen, Heikki, Elisabeth Schüssler Fiorenza, R. S. Sugirtharajah, Krister Stendahl, and James Barr. *Reading the Bible in the Global Village: Helsinki.* Atlanta: Society of Biblical Literature, 2000.

Taylor, Keeanga-Yamahtta. *How We Get Free: Black Feminism and the Combahee River Collective.* Chicago: Haymarket Books, 2017.

Tinker, George E., Curtiss Paul DeYoung, Wilda C. Gafney, Leticia Guardiola-Sáenz, and Frank Yamada, eds. *The Peoples' Bible.* Minneapolis: Fortress Press, 2008.

Traister, Rebecca. *Good and Mad: The Revolutionary Power of Women's Anger.* New York: Simon & Schuster, 2018.

Twiss, Richard. *Rescuing The Gospel From the Cowboys: A Native American Expression of the Jesus Way.* Downers Grove: InterVarsity Press, 2015.

Ukpong, Justin S., Musa W. Dube, Gerald O. West, Alpheus Masoga, Norman K. Gottwald, Jeremy Punt, Tinyiko S. Maluleke, and Vincent L. Wimbush. *Reading the Bible in the Global Village: Cape Town.* Atlanta: Society of Biblical Literature, 2002.

Wilkerson, Isabel. *The Warmth of Other Suns: The Epic Story of America's Great Migration.* New York: Random House, 2010.

Woodley, Randy S. *Shalom and the Community of Creation: An Indigenous Vision.* Grand Rapids: Wm. B. Eerdmans Publishing Company, 2012.

ONLINE RESOURCES

Bible Odyssey
   www.bibleodyssey.org

Black Lives Matter: A Reading List
   www.left-bank.com/black-lives-matter

Guide to the Chinese in California Virtual Collection
   www.oac.cdlib.org/findaid/ark:/13030/kt5p3019m2

Martin Luther King, Jr. Research & Education Institute
   kinginstitute.stanford.edu

Sacred Conversations to End Racism
   www.ucc.org/sacred_conversations_to_end_racism

STEP Bible
   www.stepbible.org

The Salt Collective
   www.thesaltcollective.org

The Urgency of Intersectionality
   www.ted.com/talks/kimberle_crenshaw_the_
   urgency_of_intersectionality

Why Treaties Matter
   www.treatiesmatter.org

ORGANIZATIONS

Antiracism Study Dialogues Circles
   www.asdicircle.org

Asian Americans Advancing Justice
   www.advancingjustice-aajc.org

Crossroads Antiracism Organizing & Training
   www.crossroadsantiracism.org

Living Justice Press
   www.livingjusticepress.org

National Congress of American Indians
   www.ncai.org

Samuel DeWitt Proctor Conference
   sdpconference.org

Showing Up for Racial Justice
   www.showingupforracialjustice.org

The People's Institute for Survival and Beyond
   www.pisab.org